Reflection and the College Teacher

A Solution for Higher Education

A Volume in
Innovative Perspectives of Higher Education:
Research, Theory, and Practice

Series Editor
Kathleen P. King, University of South Florida

Innovative Perspectives of Higher Education: Research, Theory, and Practice

Kathleen P. King, Series Editor

The Professor's Guide to Taming Technology:
Leveraging Digital Media, Web 2.0, and More for Learning (2011)
edited by Kathleen P. King and Thomas D. Cox

Pathways to Transformation: Learning in Relationship (2012)
edited by Carrie J. Boden McGill and Sola M. Kippers

Reflection and the College Teacher: A Solution for Higher Education (2014)
by Rachel Wlodarsky and Howard Walters

Reflection and the College Teacher

A Solution for Higher Education

by

Rachel Wlodarsky and Howard Walters
Ashland University

Information Age Publishing, Inc.
Charlotte, North Carolina • www.infoagepub.com

Library of Congress Cataloging-in-Publication Data

CIP data for this book can be found on the Library of Congress website
http://www.loc.gov/index.html

Paperback: 978-1-62396-469-6
Hardcover: 978-1-62396-470-2
E-Book: 978-1-62396-471-9

Printed in the United States of America

DEDICATION

I dedicate this book to my mom, in spirit; she gave me the courage, strength and wisdom to write this book. I want to thank my family-my husband Walt and our three daughters, Ella, Karin and Taylor for their support and patience as I spent long hours away from them preparing this manuscript. I also want to thank my colleague and friend, Howard Walters, for his desire to work with me on this project; the book is an enhanced resource for educators and other professionals because of our strong belief in the importance of reflection and our joint expertise as educators and researchers.

—Rachel Wlodarsky

I would additionally like to acknowledge the encouragement and support of his wife, Paula, through the difficult early career stages where time is so tight. She has enabled this work and shares in its completion.

—Howard Walters

CONTENTS

FOREWORD

Higher education would seem to be a culture of reflection and contempla-tion. In our busy lives, we sometimes put those two things on the back burner to deal with later. The focus of this monograph is on the key con-cept of reflection, both personal and professional. The authors take us to the beginning and develop the definition and conceptualization of reflec-tion. By setting the context in higher education, they create a focus on reflecting on what it is to be a teacher and professor in one of the less examined areas of education.

The first chapter, context of higher education, should be required reading for all department chairs, faculty mentors, deans, and anyone who evaluates faculty members. The combination of historical and philo-sophical with the very real everyday tensions makes the chapter useful on its own and critical for understanding the focus of the remainder of the volume.

The second chapter focuses on the questions: Refection: what is it and how has it been discussed? It deals well with taking the reader to the ques-tion when too many do not really realize it is a question. As with too many words and concepts, we have a tendency to define something as itself. This chapter will take the reader into the nature of reflection. The added element in the chapter is the clear and challenging discussion of the rela-tionship between reflection and teaching. The reader will come away knowing that this is no simple concept, but it is vital.

Chapter 3 continues the study of reflection and college teaching. The culture is not very reflective. The activity of reflection seems to speak of nar-cissism and that is not an attractive concept in higher education. The authors separate the two concepts—reflection is a valuable activity and requires training and practice. The event path that is posited is a useful and practical tool that is consistent with the intellectual reality of reflection. The integration of reflection with teaching is even clearer in the chapter.

Reflection and the College Teacher: A Solution for Higher Education
pp. xi–xii
Copyright © 2014 by Information Age Publishing

Building on the preceding chapters, Chapter 4 focuses on the event path. The combination of clear delineation of process and the relationship of the process to college teaching gives strength to the arguments presented earlier. The use of cognition as a problem-defining tool and the presentation of "tools" as data collection provide a platform for defining the "change point" as planning for the future. Bringing the process full circle, the new event details the new behavior and begins the cycle again.

The "event" is a key element in the reflection process and Chapter 5 provides both definition and clarity. The language of authenticity and the inclusion of phenomenology frame the discussion and, as the authors say, provide the bedrock of the interaction of learning in and through practice. Definition and usage continue with the discussion of cognition in Chapter 6. The ties between practice and theory are clear and useful.

Chapter 7 is the "toolkit." The identification of critical reflective tools and the use of these tools provide a focus for the reader and helps build a better toolbox for the college teacher. It is a central element of the chapter that the tool must be clearly thought out and the characteristics of each tool have to be understood. The praxis elements here are very clear and very thoughtful.

How and where does one change? What leads up to that point? Chapter 8 brings together the concepts, knowledge, and skills discussed earlier and highlight the change point where behavior changes consciously. The clear tie between cognition and changed behavior is described and the implications are logically developed. The relationship between event—cognition—new event is clearly presented with excellent examples from real life.

Chapter 9 brings all of the chapters together. The title "Reflection in Action in Higher Education" brings the reader back to context. The elegance of the path is clear and the focus on praxis is a wonderful way to end the journey the monograph outlines.

I would encourage every faculty member to read and to think about the idea of reflection as presented by our authors. It will help layout a rewarding and profitable journey.

—Ann Converse Shelly
Immediate Past President, Association of Teacher Educators

ACKNOWLEDGMENTS

Ten years ago, as new faculty members, we sat staring (metaphorically) at the promotion and tenure guidelines and requirements for our college and university. The overwhelming tasks of learning new, assigned courses and learning the ropes of committee service on campus were overwhelming. The additional need to engage and move forward with our respective and collective research agendas appeared as an incomprehensible task.

We engaged with that work load and were successful, as evidenced by this book, our continued success as now senior faculty members, and by the layers of prior research that anticipated this volume. But that work was not done in isolation and without the support of many colleagues and friends who gave time and interest to our careers and this work.

At the outset of the research studies on faculty reflection that we will reference in this book, we solicited the feedback from a select group of senior faculty members here at Ashland University. These individuals— nameless here as most ultimately participated in our data collection activities—not only provided meaningful feedback, but actively encouraged us to move forward, challenged us to think more deeply and write more critically, and even urged us to challenge the system appropriately to see the work completed. We are deeply thankful for this group of leaders and colleagues in our college.

As we have published individual manuscripts and smaller studies over this decade, we have had many other colleagues at the American Association for Adult and Continuing Education and the Commission of Professors of Adult Education, as well as at the Association for Teacher Education who have attended our paper presentations. These colleagues have written us comments, have asked key and penetrating questions, and have challenged our thinking over the years. As we have refined and

Reflection and the College Teacher: A Solution for Higher Education
pp. xiii–xiv

directed our research forward, these colleagues and those professional associations have been invaluable.

Finally, we would be remiss in not explicitly thanking our friend and colleague Dr. Carl Walley for his critical comments and editing expertise as we finalized this manuscript. His support and work have been greatly beneficial to us.

CHAPTER 1

COLLEGES OF EDUCATION IN 21ST CENTURY AMERICA

In his groundbreaking novel *Jude the Obscure*, Thomas Hardy has his pro-
tagonist, the young boy Jude Fawley, climb a workman's ladder to the top
of a barn early in the story. From the vantage point of the barn at sunset,
Jude, watching the sun reflect from the windows of the cathedral at the
University at Christminster, contemplates a life of scholarship, of matricu-
lation at the university. Hardy (1970) wrote:

> It is a city of light, he said to himself.... The tree of knowledge grows there,
> he added a few steps further on.... It is a place that teachers of men spring
> from and go to.... It is what you may call a castle, manned by scholarship
> and religion. After this figure, he was silent a long while, till he added.... It
> would suit me just well. (p. 19)

Indeed, these youthful and lofty conceptions of the university, its students, its faculty, and its ambiance frame many people's conceptions of
the approximately 7,000 colleges and universities in the United States,
even today. They are places somewhat ethereal, with esteemed reputa-
tions for seriousness, for academic rigor, that are essentially unbounded
by the laws of business; places of near-pious intellectualism and fervor.

Increasingly in the United States, however, many people are drawing
quite different conclusions about the role, purpose, and effect of the institutions of higher education that populate and plague our communities.

Reflection and the College Teacher: A Solution for Higher Education
pp. 1–9
Copyright © 2014 by Information Age Publishing
All rights of reproduction in any form reserved.

To read any current media coverage of education in America is to quickly encounter a level of criticism bordering on near-contempt, given that the accusations and attacks are leveled at institutions historically central to the founding and development of this nation, and central to the continued creation and sustenance of many professional fields and academic communities on which the nation depends.

Teachers and teacher educators are caricatured beyond recognition in some circles and on some news channels and in ways which, were these depictions even half-truthful, should result in legal indictments, much less educational reform. As we write this opening chapter of a book intended to refine and improve colleges of education and similar organizations, our local newspaper continues to focus on executive and legislative challenges to teacher professional autonomy, playing out in Wisconsin, Ohio, Indiana, Michigan, and many other states in our Midwestern region and across the nation generally. Taken together, many of these attacks follow the narrative that teachers in K-12 classrooms and colleges of education are nearly entirely self-serving, interested only in their salary and benefits, and lacking in empathy and compassion for their respective charges.

It is not our intent to pile on to the accusations nor to rebut them. We do acknowledge that this is the social context of our practice, however. We are faculty members within a college of education which, as they all do, has strengths and weaknesses, positive and negative attributes. We choose to situate ourselves philosophically in an attitude of constant growth and improvement, of a never-ending cycle of reform, revisioning, and reinvigoration. We hold to a perspective that "a table is a dead tree that needs dusting" and that as long as a tree lives, it grows, it changes, it extends its reach. So, too, colleges of education and the college teachers who inhabit them. As long as they live, they need to grow, change, and extend their reach. Our book intends to discuss one particular construct, personal and professional reflection, as a means toward growth and change. Not as a hammer to further critique and caricature these hardworking and well-intentioned colleagues, but as a constructive approach to helping.

Nevertheless, to best set the context of why continued growth and change is critical and necessary, we think it helpful to provide a concise overview of six pressures that are faced by colleges of education in the current contexts in which they function. As we will revisit at the end of this book, a disposition and enhanced capacity to be reflective, individually and collectively, will provide an enhanced strength to withstand and mitigate these pressures, and to envision a path through this gauntlet that ensures colleges of education a continued role in societal leadership.

SOCIETAL CONCEPTIONS OF COLLEGE FACULTY

Recently, there has been a call for greater accountability and a nationwide investment in assessing and documenting the outcomes of education (Levine, 2010). As a result universities have refocused their attention on teaching and the instructional performance of college teachers. According to DeWaters and Baiocco (1998), because faculty are the infantry, attacking the problems on the front lines within colleges and universities, it can be argued that faculty development is the key to reform. As part of their professional role, faculty are responsible for analyzing, synthesizing, evaluating, and communicating the changes that are occurring not only in their respective disciplines, but also in society.

This refocus on college teaching is not without precedent. Boyer (1990) led a challenge to traditional conceptions of the work of college faculty with his model of scholarship, which has become ubiquitous in higher education faculty literature. His notion of the *scholarship of teaching* permeates the global community, and is the framework for large-scale quality assurance programs around the world (Macfarlane & Ottewill, 2004; Strydom, Zulu, & Murray, 2004).

Schuster (2003) contributed a concise rationale for the importance of this focus on faculty teaching in higher education:

> The focus on actual student learning has been neglected. Put another way, for far too long presumptions of educational quality were linked to input measures ... such as the academic degrees of the faculty, the size of the library, the institutional endowment, and standardized scores of entering students ... [there is a belated awareness] that such inputs are not the best potential measures of educational effectiveness and have little bearing on how well students learn. (p. 17)

Schuster continued (p.16) that "the stakes are higher today" in higher education, with strictures on funding, greater competition among non-traditional providers and pressures from the global marketplace. He concluded this essay with the observation that "higher education is currently experiencing more profound changes in a shorter span of time than has ever been the case" (p. 17). McNaught (2003, pp. 18-19) described these changes as in part "being required to educate more students, from an increasing variety of backgrounds, with decreasing government funding; they [colleges] are required to compete vigorously for student enrollments and external sources of funding." Altogether, the faculty's capacity to manage these pressures maximizes the importance that the faculty becomes critically reflective of its role, its practice, and its goals in the academy.

PHILOSOPHICAL TENSION SURROUNDING TEACHER EDUCATION

Against this social backdrop where the role and autonomy of college teachers is questioned and contested, colleges of education continue their historic struggle with the philosophical definition at the core of their very identity: Is teacher education fundamentally an academic activity, or fundamentally a clinical activity, or somewhere in between? This discussion has been most clearly elucidated in Levine's report (2010) that positioned this as a nearly insurmountable dichotomy contesting the very soul of the college of education. Levine termed this debate the "profession/craft" debate and described it as a political struggle internal to colleges of education, but playing out in a social context that is equally ambiguous. Levine argues that, the United States lacks a common vision of how to prepare teachers to meet today's new realities, leading to the rise of divergent and opposing approaches to reform. This is a powerful argument, but falls well short of describing the civil wars that rage among the faculty at many colleges of education over the implications of curricular choices, technology integration, and generational and cultural discourses that vary across newer and seasoned professors. The lack of clear vision in society is only mirrored in colleges of education, begging the "chicken or the egg" questions: could society better understand and buy into a compelling and unified vision of teacher training if only college teachers responsible for this activity could find such a vision for themselves? And what does the near future look like as civil discourse gives way to raw exercises in political power of the sort we have recently observed in the Midwest United States? How do we triangulate a position that rejects narrow assumptions and generalizations on both ends of the political spectrum, taking the high road of academic excellence, intellectual honesty, and ethical practice that centralizes social good for all of our citizens, from the least to the greatest?

BUDGET PRESSURES

Were these first external pressures on colleges of education all we had on our plates, we could likely agree that intelligent systems, processes, institutions and faculty would eventually find tractable solutions to, at least, triangulate to a central, consensus position. Unfortunately, time may not allow the luxury of incremental discourse necessary to find consensus. Two budget realities seem to conspire at the moment to force all of our hands on a time-table that none would normally accept as reasonable. First, the historic "cash cow" relationship of colleges of education to their universities is increasingly threatened by demographic changes in the

United States. As the historic cash flows associated to colleges of education decline, the relative insulation of these colleges from institutional realities and pressures is quickly dissolving. At our own institution, the masters in education program at its height accounted for nearly 10% of university tuition revenue. New faculty positions were added nearly as fast as hiring committees could move through the process. Automatic budget lines for professional travel, for department supply budgets, for clerical support were built into annual budgets and generally not questioned. Now, through federal and state policy changes, challenges to the master's degree model roll down to the budget in our small institution, with direct implications on faculty work and support. These structural changes are only exacerbated by the shifting political winds wherein the professional fields of education associated themselves to a single political party, and as that party waxes and wanes over the election cycle, so does the political and governmental support for the professions. Policy and programming decisions that decades ago were incremental and driven at a snail's pace as theory and practice kept a rough pace with each other are now driven, not by emerging theoretical discourse, but by a dialectic of ideology, and on two-year and four-year election cycles and response times. As these election cycles produce changes in the political discourse concerned with teacher preparation, licensure, and accountability, the pressures on colleges of education, and the budget implications to colleges of education, increase.

The second substantive budgetary pressure on colleges of education is derived from the increasingly precarious state of affairs in federal and state government budgets (Anderson & McGreal, 2012; Sack, 2005). All things being equal, education is not the most powerful voice at the federal and state budget tables. Health care, safety and security issues such as military, police, fire, and prison systems, and downward pressure on public budgets from pension and retirement costs compete with education systems for budgetary attention. Such pressure is only expected to increase, with recent reports from the Office of Management of the Budget suggesting that the nondiscretionary portion of the federal budget, by conservative estimates, is likely to further contract annually over the next decade.

TECHNOLOGY PRESSURES

In describing classrooms in the United States collectively, Wise and Rothman (2010, p. 52) note "American classrooms are not significantly different from what they were early in the last century." Continuing, they noted, "In just about every other facet of society, technology has transformed the way Americans go about their lives. Yet schools have been slow to embrace the transformative power of technology."

These descriptions are as true of higher education classrooms, and sometimes much more so, than the K-12 classrooms in this country. Nevertheless, as productivity software, social media, and innovative hardware and computing devices have proliferated, college classrooms are increasingly isolated from the digital revolution shaping national and global culture. Some of this isolation is rooted in conceptualizations of the role and function of professors, in some critical ways, we are the content of the course, and some of the isolation is rooted in financial limitations, cultural histories, and the challenges of change (Anderson & McGreal, 2012).

The gap between higher education classrooms and the digital world results in conceptions of colleges of education as "being behind" the K-12 classrooms for which they purport to be preparing practitioners. These conceptions may have a basis in fact. This gap also creates appropriate political ammunition for policymakers and the public to question the broader relevance of colleges of education as the gatekeepers for America's classroom professionals.

GLOBALIZATION

From the earliest roots of American education and teacher education, the link between the role of the classroom teacher and the creation of productive citizens for the nation has been at the forefront of vision and policy statements for education institutions and agencies. What has changed dramatically and in ways most unanticipated is the changing conception of citizenship and national identity. In the edited text *The Future of Citizenship* (Ciprut, 2008), a series of eminent researchers and essayists delved into the emerging postnationalistic and global constructs for citizenship which threaten, and in fact are, turning on its head the historic, national perspective of citizenship in its historic form. In the opening essay, Ciprut wrote,

> Globalization as a force of change … has created a mosaic of social, economic, and political spaces that transcend and weaken the political boundaries of physical space. That very force of change goes up against today's idea of citizenship based on the moral and legal claims of the Westphalian territorial state. (p.17)

Consequently, students in today's higher education classrooms are frequently not U.S. citizens. For those many who are, the generation of students in today's college classrooms increasingly communicate, seamlessly, with peers, mentors, friends, and family across the globe as easily as they communicate with individuals in their own hometowns. Young adults have a view of the world the same as Thomas Friedman (2005) does: flat, connected, and integrated. They contemplate international travel and study, and international internships at transnational corporations. In our own college, we routinely place student teachers in international student teaching experiences to complete their licensure programs for initial teacher certification. It is nearly as easy to contemplate finding a first teaching job abroad as in our own communities, and sometimes easier.

These realities create curricular pressures, among other pressures. To what extent do we prepare students, as eventual classroom teachers, for the global community? Increasingly, most teachers encounter students for whom English is not the first or only language. Increasingly, most teachers will need to negotiate non-Western cultural traditions in the classroom. Eventually, professional licensure as a teacher may require non-Western, global experiences (Apple, Kenway, & Singh, 2005). How will this space be created in very thick, 4-year baccalaureate degree programs?

ACADEMY ISSUES

The final issue confronting colleges of education is an amalgam of interrelated phenomena we label Academy Issues. These issues are highly contextual: some readers may have an entirely different list of these struggles from their context that another reader may not recognize. We will simply suggest some of the tensions and issues in this area that we have observed at the, now, six different higher education institutions in which we have worked in our careers.

First, within the college of education, students have historically appreciated faculty who possess rich stories from their own experiences as practitioners in the field of education, either as classroom teachers, administrators, or both. For many years, the faculty of what became the college of education, were drawn from the ranks of senior administrators and classroom teachers. Labaree (2004), in his historical treatment of colleges of education, *The Trouble with Ed Schools* (2004), provided a well-articulated background on this history. The reality of this history is still with us. Frequently, professors in colleges of education lack the scholarly credentials and strengths that are required in other colleges, and this rolls downhill with respect to the overall perception of the college of education in the academy. There remains a cultural tension in many hiring committees in colleges of education regarding appropriate credentials. Do foundations faculty, for example, need K-12 classroom experience, or solid research and doctoral coursework in the content? Where is the balance in this dichotomy?

A second academy issue is the tension between teaching, research and service. In our experience, even if the college of education has worked out the balance between these three, there is nearly always a "first among equals" approach to teaching evaluations over research productivity. Again, even if the college of education has worked out a balance internally, the degree to which this balance is shared, communicated, and accepted by the broader university is an utterly different issue.

A third academy issue is the tension between quality control among students, and the institutional budget or fiscal codependency between colleges of education and their universities. Let us speak frankly: most colleges of education, and particularly MEd programs, have been at some point or other the "cash cows" of their institutions. This of course fluctuates depending on the various state requirements for classroom teachers to obtain continuing education credit or advanced degrees. Nevertheless, many colleges of education are possessed of large MEd populations that generate substantial revenue streams on which many institutional budget lines rest. The back pressure to maintain enrollment, even if that means compromising on admissions' standards, is palpable. Faculty are appropriately concerned with the number of adjunct faculty required to cover core course sections and enrollments, but decreasing enrollment has far-reaching institutional budget implications. In a perfect world, some of the choices made decades ago would not have been made, but those bridges are crossed, and the interrelationship between college of education enrollment and the broader budget cannot be easily unwound.

Finally, the stress of managing field supervision, where this is built into the load requirements in the professional school, creates a tension between the faculty who are responsible for licensure programs and field requirements and those faculty, frequently graduate faculty, who are "only" responsible for classroom instruction. These two communities frequently do not communicate well, or at all, and many colleges of education are de facto comprised of an undergraduate and graduate faculty who rarely communicate, cooperate, or collaborate. In addition, they are frequently at odds with each other over load issues, credit allocation for core courses and methods courses, and over resource allocation.

IMPLICATIONS

Amid all of these issues and tensions, and many more that could have been mentioned, how does a college faculty manage the multiple flows of information, competing interests and expectations, and programmatic and structural dichotomies? What are the answers?

We don't even pretend to know. We do know that reflection is a tool with great power to align and clarify these tensions, and to, at least reveal management and planning solutions, coping strategies, and reasonable avenues of attack. Becoming reflective practitioners, as professors in colleges of education, will allow us to not only model the strategy we teach and expect of our students, but to also gain a better understanding in the "first person" of how better to create these types of professionals in the second tier: among our own graduates. In a nutshell, that is the purpose of this book. We should be that which we expect our students to be: reflective learners, able to note our authentic life experiences, learn from these experiences, and chart a forward path of change that demonstrates we can hold on to the best practices and decisions while avoiding an endless and repeated cycle of error.

Through the remainder of this book, using a framework we established in our research over the past decade, we will present an experience and action driven pathway for reflective driven decision making in the environment of a college of education. Following an overall presentation of the model, we disaggregate the reflective path into its segments, and at the conclusion of each of these chapters, provide the individual professor with a set of guiding questions to consider how she or he might address the chapter contents in professional practice. Further, we provide a set of questions, which may be rhetorical or could be addressed in practice, and that are oriented to the college of education as a unit. It is hoped these questions might challenge the college to undertake a unitwide or system-wide reinvention of itself around the construct of reflective decision making and action. Our final chapter analyzes the college as a unit, and considers the place and function, and potentiality of reflective decision-making in guiding structural and system-level activity in the college.

CHAPTER 2

WHAT IS REFLECTION, ITS CAPACITY, AND WHY IS IT IMPORTANT?

Kathy Burton was a midcareer faculty member in her college of education. Opinionated, determined, and idealistic, Burton began her career as a teacher of special needs children where she was instrumental in building an award-winning intervention program for students with severe behavioral disorders. After 8 years and nearly burning out from emotional and physical exhaustion, she returned to school herself, obtaining her doctorate in special education from a solid, Midwestern university. With successful classroom experience and a doctorate in a critical need area, she quickly found herself recruited into a tenure-track position in a college of education. The recruitment experience included campus visits, lunch with attentive potential colleagues, and wine with the chair in the evening. This was intoxicating after years of thankless service in the trenches of the special needs classroom and her graduate school budget. She had no second thoughts about accepting the offer that soon followed her interview.

Arriving on campus was a marriage without a honeymoon for Burton. Shifting interests from senior faculty and an unexpected vacancy over the summer produced a first semester schedule of four different course preparations, and the young professor began to understand the meaning of a "twelve/twelve" load for the first time. Yet the energy of the students, and her own passion for making a difference in the direction of the field in a more profound and impactful way by leveraging her influence over groups of future special needs teachers made for a highly satisfying first semester. Her own energy and fresh perspective carried over into her classes,

Reflection and the College Teacher: A Solution for Higher Education
pp. 11–31

where student evaluations noted her cutting edge knowledge, the obvious experi-ence she brought as a "real" special needs expert, and the rigor of the course.

Second semester began much like the first, although her schedule began to settle in a bit more. She discovered the concept of "cohort programs" and off-site delivery so typical in colleges of education, and found herself driving to evening classes delivered in adjoining counties at regional high schools, in addition to her campus classes.

By midspring when she met with her chair for her annual review meeting, she typed her annual report with a small but growing sense of being unfinished. Her classes had gone well, at least as measured by her student evaluations. There were certainly organizational areas to improve, but that was a given for first-years. It was the scholarship that was a sudden, glaring, empty spot in her report. Where had the year gone? How could she possibly have managed her time differently to make space for writing or, more still, for expanding the research line she had begun in her dissertation? And why, even when colleagues told her to "just focus on your teaching the first year" did she have the sense that something was not quite right with her progress. And beyond the annual report form, was there some way to be more systematic, personal, and self-focused in her introspection and self-monitor-ing? Was there a way to connect her authentic self, complete with her own goals for professional and personal integration, with the more immediate and compelling demands of the college in which she was now embedded?

CENTRAL ISSUE OF THE CHAPTER

This chapter is designed to describe reflection and its capacity and explain how the process can empower a college faculty, individually and collectively, to move toward an enhanced capability of meeting the social and professional responsibilities of the organization. As we have studied reflection and professional practice among college faculty over the past several years, it has become clear to us that reflection can be a force for self-improvement for professors and also for colleges overall. The prob-lems, concerns, challenges and issues confronting higher education in the United States, as discussed in Chapter 1, can find immediate and longer term structural relief if colleges capture the spirit of authentic reflective practice and channel that toward systemic and meaningful improvement.

To do this, we must move beyond platitudes about reflection and deeply consider its historic and intellectual roots. Is reflection more than "thinking about" some experience we have gone through? Is it evaluating performance and designing interventions to mitigate past deficiencies? Is reflection essentially a cognitive process, to result in an objectified analy-sis of practice for the faculty portfolio or annual review and never to meaningfully result in personal or collective change? Is it something we do to satisfy an accrediting body, or is it a deeply held core value that we foreground in practice? Does the degree to which one has the capacity to reflect vary? To work out answers to these questions, we begin with a selection of the literature around the concept of reflection as a way to deduce a core definition of the term or concept, on which we will build toward a more pragmatic system of faculty growth in later chapters.

THE CENTRALITY OF FACULTY

Current research on higher education shows an increasing recognition that the faculty are at the center of any attempt to improve the quality of teaching and learning. Attempts to reorganize programs, develop curriculum, and improve faculty effectiveness ultimately rely on the professional development of individual faculty members. As we have studied college faculty over the last decade, we have increasingly come to perceive that *critical reflection* may facilitate the process of making implicit beliefs explicit, allowing for these individual faculty members to develop, reflect, and enhance their classroom practices, and to consequently improve the outcomes of higher education for students.

SUPPORT FROM RESEARCH

Both our research and that of others supports the relevance and criticality of reflective practice in professional development programs both for college faculty (Hatala [Wlodarsky], 2002; Wlodarsky, 2005) and for K-12 classroom teachers (Walters, 2002). Findings suggest:

1. that reflection can, but may not, lead to changes in practice;
2. that reflective practice is a multidimensional process, and
3. that reflective practice includes discreet skills which may be taught and learned (Day, 1993; Feiman-Nemser & Parker, 1992; Ferry & Ross-Gordon, 1998; Hoffman-Kipp, Artiles, & Lopez-Torres, 2003; Schön, 1987; Usher, Bryant, & Johnston, 1997).

In this vein, we have found that reflection among college faculty members can be linked to changed beliefs and practices in their classrooms. Beginning in 2004, we collected qualitative and quantitative data to describe the nature and characteristics of reflective practice in an typical college setting, and quantitative data to test the associative strength of these characteristics with select demographic variables identified in the literature and collected by the researchers to describe education faculty members.

BACKGROUND AND HISTORY OF REFLECTIVE PRACTICE

When Schön (1987) discussed the "ill-defined problems of practice" associated with professional life, he may well have been writing about the professional lives of teacher educators. Added to the problems associated with accreditation, compliance, and licensure, teacher educators have the task-derived decisions associated with daily job responsibilities around teaching, curriculum, and state standards. Decisions concerning time-management, priority setting, and student complexity are ill-defined, stressful, and fraught with ambiguity. Added to these, the compounded struggles with institutional tenure requirements, the technical and rhetorical requirements for publication and conference presentation, and committee service seem overwhelming. How can these teacher educators and college faculty members survive the pressures of professional, personal and societal requirements? One answer to this question is the application of *reflection on practice* as a self-directed approach to professional development and personal life management. In Dewey's words (1933),

> Reflection emancipates us from merely impulsive and merely routine activity, it enables us to direct our activities with foresight and to plan according to ends-in-view or purposes of that we are aware, to act in deliberate and intentional fashion, to know what we are about when we act. (p. 17)

For Dewey (1933, p. 78), a fundamental purpose of education is to help people acquire habits of reflection so they can engage in intelligent action.

Ball and Cohen (1999) argued that the vision of a better education is complex, therefore; teachers need opportunities to reconsider their current practices and to examine others, as well as to learn more about the subjects and students they teach (as cited in Darling-Hammond & Sykes, 1999). *Reflection* would facilitate such opportunities.

Reflective practice has been found to be both relevant and valuable in the professional development of both college teachers and K-12 classroom teachers. One of the authors (Wlodarsky, 2005) found that reflection, in particular, among teacher educators can be related to changed beliefs and practices in their classrooms. Other studies have also suggested that reflection can lead to positive changes in practice (Ferry & Ross-Gordon, 1998; Hoffman-Kipp et al., 2003; Schön, 1987). These studies suggest that, given the current and emerging need to address learning and performance outcomes in the higher education arena, reflection and reflective practice by teacher educators is worth intensive focus. This focus will aid understanding of what may be a very practical and underappreciated approach to enhancing the outcomes of a college of education.

CHRONOLOGICAL OVERVIEW OF THE CONCEPT OF REFLECTION

The definition and purpose of reflection is an evolving conceptual idea that changes and emerges as we review the literature. The literature on reflective practice summarized below provides a chronological overview of these evolving definitions and purposes.

The notion of reflection has been studied for almost a century, beginning with John Dewey. It was Dewey who first linked his findings on reflection to the profession of education. Dewey (1933) identified the need for teachers, in particular, to reflect on their practices in order to act deliberately and intentionally rather than spontaneously and routinely. Dewey (1933) and Schön (1987) contended that teachers' work is complex and requires deep and foundational reflective practices.

In ancient Latin and French terms, reflection connoted "bending back" on oneself. In contemporary terms, Seibert and Daudelin (1999) related reflection to the mental activity individuals engage in to try to make sense of experience.

Freire (1973) believed reflection resulted in critical consciousness in that learners become actors, not observers, and authors of their own decisions. When we as learners fail to reflect on our place in the world or critically evaluate the validity of information presented to us, we become passive and superficial, accepting faulty logic, untested ideas and allow ourselves to be swayed by deceptive arguments and polemics. Freire argued, by combining action and reflection, we create *praxis*—a set of practices informed by reflection. Thus our actions are not random or haphazard but informed and deliberate and we are aware of why we do what we do.

Boud, Keogh, and Walker (1985) described reflection as "a generic term for those intellectual and affective activities in that individuals engage to explore their experiences in order to lead to new understandings and appreciations" (p. 19). Richards (1990) argued "reflection is a response to a past experience and involves conscious recall and examination of the experience as a basis for evaluation and decision making and as a source for planning and action" (p. 5).

Twenty years later, Freire (1993) discussed the concept of reflection, once again. This time he described reflection as "an objectification of experience in time, epochs of past, present, and future that allows a human being to plan for a different future" (p. 83).

Mezirow (1991) differentiated among three types of reflection on experience, only one of which, *premise reflection*, can lead to transformative learning. Premise reflection involves examining long-held, socially constructed assumptions, beliefs and values about an experience or problem. He also made a distinction between reflection being implicit, as when we mindlessly choose between good and evil because of our assimilated values, or explicit, as when we bring the process of choice into awareness to examine and assess the reasons for making a choice (Mezirow, 1998).

Atkins and Murphy (1995) defined reflection in the professional arena as a complex and deliberate process of thinking about and interpreting experience in order to learn from it. Imel (1992) added, "reflective practice links thought and action, because its objective is to improve one's professional practice. Reflective thinking has also been defined by Mahnaz (1997) in relationship to metacognition as "thinking about one's own thinking." He argued that this was self-monitoring based on cognitive-mediational theories of learning.

In *Teaching and Learning Through Critical Reflective Practice*, Ghaye and Ghaye (1998) defined reflection as "looking back and making sense of your practice, learning this and using this learning to affect your future action; it is about making sense of your professional life" (p. 2). More specifically, these authors spoke of ten principles that exist within the notion of reflective practice, these include:

1. Reflective practice needs to be understood as a discourse.
2. Reflective practice is fuelled and energized by experience,.
3. Reflective practice is a process that involves a reflective turn; this means returning to look again at all our taken-for-granted values, professional understandings and practices,
4. Reflective practice is concerned with learning how to account for ourselves.
5. Reflective practice should be understood as a disposition to inquiry.
6. Reflective practice is interest-serving, when we reflect we are engaging in a process of knowledge creation.
7. Reflective practice is enacted by those who are critical thinkers.
8. Reflective practice is a way of decoding a symbolic landscape.
9. Reflective practice sits at the interface between notions of practice and theory.

10.   Reflective practice occupies a position at the confluence or inter-section of a number of ways of knowing (pp. 16-19).

More recently, Brookfield (2000) concurred that Mezirow's argument for premise or critical reflection is central to transformative learning and went a step further by defining critical reflection as some sort of power analysis involving hegemonic assumptions. Jay and Johnson (2002) provided a similar description of the reflective process:

> Reflection is a process, both individual and collaborative, involving experi-ence and uncertainty. It is comprised of identifying questions and key ele-ments of a matter that have emerged as significant, then taking one's thoughts into dialogue with oneself and others. One evaluates insights gained from the process with reference to: (1) additional perspectives, (2) one's own values, experiences and beliefs, and (3) the larger context within which the questions are raised. (p. 76)

As Feinstein (2004) noted, critical reflection and reflective discourse "are two processes that are used to facilitate transformative learning; without these processes, it is unlikely that an action of learning will be truly trans-formative" (p. 109).

Merriam (2004) added to the complexity of reflection by introducing levels of maturation for reflection. Merriam argued that,

> being able to critically reflect and in particular, to critically self-reflect on our own assumptions as well as those of others, that involves critique of a premise upon that which the learner has defined as a problem mandates an advanced level of cognitive development. (p. 116)

In addition to the field of education, the concept of reflection has also been studied within numerous other professional arenas, Seibert and Daudelin (1999) observed,

> There is considerable literature from scholars in education, law, nursing and medicine focusing on professional practice. From these perspectives, reflec-tion is seen as an ongoing process of critically examining current and past professional practices against standards or objectives with the goal of improving future practices and increasing knowledge. (p. 2)

When several of the concepts of reflection are viewed in combination, a stronger understanding of reflection is gained; therefore reviewing and synthesizing these numerous definitions and/or views of reflection may provide a comfort level in that professionals choose to proceed with the reflective process.

REFLECTION IN THE EDUCATION PROFESSIONS

The question still remains, how can education faculty be good reflective practitioners if they do not completely understand what the concept "reflection" means? Part of the problem, according to Kuit, Reay, and Freeman (2001), is that the term itself is open to many interpretations. In everyday conversation, it has been devalued to describe merely thinking about a subject without the element of query and inquiry. Nevertheless, many researchers have made efforts to develop a better understanding of reflective practice specific to the profession of teaching.

Dewey (1933) and Schön (1987) argued for a proactive and learner-centered form of reflection in that the teacher becomes the owner of, and subject in, the process of his or her own reflection. This would result in developing a language for talking and thinking about their own practices, questioning the sometimes contradictory beliefs underpinning their practice, and taking greater control over their own professional growth. Schön (1987) argued that reflective practice is "a research process in that the fruits of reflection are used to challenge and reconstruct individual and collective teacher action" (as cited in Ghaye & Ghaye, 1998, p. 5). According to Mezirow (1998), "a reflective teacher is one who, given particular circumstances, is able to distance herself from the world in that she is an everyday participant and open herself to influence by others" (as cited in Loughran, 1999, p. 218).

Shulman (1987) defined reflection as a teacher's recalling the teaching and learning experience, reconstructing the events, generating alternatives, and considering the ethical implications of the teaching event. Reflection is also referred to as critical reflection, an activity or process in that experience is recalled, considered, and evaluated, usually in relation to a broader purpose. Grimmett, MacKinnon, Earickson, and Riecken (1990) believe reflection is a more deliberate process that asks teachers to question their understandings, rethink their assumptions, and consider their options.

Zeichner and Tabachnick (1991, as cited in Zeichner, 1994) identified four varieties of reflective practice in U.S. teacher education. These include *academic* that stresses subject matter, *social efficiency* emphasizing the application of teaching strategies, *developmentalist* is sensitive to students' interest, thinking and patterns of developmental growth, and *social reconstructionist* that focuses on the institutional, social, and political contexts of schooling. *Generic* reflection is defined as reflection in general that advocates, without much specificity, about the desired purposes and content of the reflection.

According to Day (1933), reflective practice is defined as continuing conscious and systematic review of the purposes, plans, action, and evaluation of teaching in order to reinforce effectiveness and, where appropriate, prompt change (as cited in Busher & Saran, 1995). Hatton and Smith (1995, as cited in Lord & Lomicka, 2007) identified essential issues concerning reflection:

> It is necessary to frame and reframe complex or ambiguous problems, test out various interpretations and then modify our actions consequently; it is important to look back systematically on our actions after they have taken place in order to extend our thoughts; while some activities are considered reflective, such as the use of journaling or group discussions following practical experiences, they may not be directed towards the solution of specific problems; and a central factor in reflection is to take into consideration the wider historic, cultural and political beliefs as we seek solution to problems. (pp. 515-516)

More recently, Kuit et al. (2001), described a reflective teacher as one who compares her teaching against her own experience and knowledge of educational theory that predicts what might happen. Invariably, these comparisons highlight differences between theory and practice, and the reflective process readjusts the theory until it accurately describes the practice. Therefore, Kuit et al (2001) argued that "reflective practice is about the process of teaching rather than about a simple evaluation of teaching, questioning why we do something rather than how, and most important of all, learning from this process" (pp. 130-131).

Lloyd (2002) argued that reflective practitioners impact their professional development by changing their perspectives about the roles of pupils and teachers in the learning process, through self-critical analysis, an acknowledgement of the need to take responsibility for changing and developing their own practices, and creating a more systematic approach to evaluating practice.

Corcoran and Leahy (2003) supported the need for teachers to have an inquiry orientation. They believe reflection is not simply a matter of thinking back on actions taken but rather effective teachers look for internal, logical consistency and inconsistency between espoused beliefs and actions taken. When describing this inquiry orientation, Corcoran and Leahy cited "Kotkamp's cycle of paying deliberate, analytical attention to one's action in relation to intentions, as if from an external observer's perspective, for the purpose of expanding one's options and making decisions about improved ways of acting in the future" (p. 32). Corcoran and Leahy further emphasized social support in reflective practice; this requires a public testing of private assumptions as well as dialogue with other participants in the teaching-learning context (Corcoran & Leahy, 2003; Leahy & Corcoran, 1996).

Reflection for professional teachers, according to Russo and Ford (2006), is an opportunity to critically evaluate practice against objectives, to see problems in the classroom as both opportunity and provocation to examine and assess the learning that is occurring. Pultorak (1993) added to the concept of reflection by arguing that reflectivity is a developmental process for novice teachers. He determined that teachers move from thinking about their teaching at the level of practice to the level of theorizing about that practice.

Despite the differing emphases in conceptions of reflective practice, there is, according to Calderhead (1992), some general agreement that the reflective teacher is one who is able to analyze his own practice and the context in that it occurs; the reflective teacher is expected to be able to stand back from his own teaching, evaluate his situation and take responsibility for his own future action.

Agreeing upon and having a better understanding of reflection may motivate teachers to actually participate in the reflective process. However, teachers must also be aware of the different tools they can use to facilitate the process effectively.

IS REFLECTION MORE THAN "THINKING ABOUT?"

One could argue that all teachers, as with all adults, *think*. However, not all teachers are equally adept at posing, analyzing, and solving problems; nor do all teachers recognize good teaching practices such that the practice can be sustainably replicated. Yet a highly developed disposition for analytical and reflective thinking promotes teacher development and contributes to enhanced student learning (Danielson, 2008).

In teacher education, reflective practice supports teachers as they move from routine actions in their teaching to more considered, cognitive actions. It is reasoned that this transformation brought about through reflection makes teachers "better" or at the very least aware of their pedagogical beliefs and practices (Vallance, 2006). Choulier, Picard, and Weite (2007, p. 115) described reflection as the attitude adopted by an individual in order to take an external and critical look at his or her activity (in progress or completed). It allows him or her to analyze the contextual and generic elements of a situation, to gain a critical distance in relationship to the schemas being used, and to capitalize on past successes and failures to create a more successful future.

According to Lyons, (2006) reflection is an intentional act of mind, engaging a person alone or in collaboration with others in interrogating one's teaching, especially a compelling or puzzling situation of teaching or learning to construct some understanding of it. Others have discussed reflective practice as an iterative process that seeks to compare teaching practice to theories of action, and to adjust practice accordingly. Thus, reflection on teaching goes beyond mere evaluation in that it involves the process, ideas, assumptions and beliefs behind the action and does not examine students' opportunities to learn merely from the perspective of products and outcomes (Bernacchio, Ross, Washburn, Whitney, & Wood, 2007; Hammersley-Fletcher & Orsmond, 2005; Kuit et al., 2001, p. 57). Other researchers do not assume that improving *how one teaches* always necessitates reflection. They do assume, however, that reflection on one's teaching is likely to raise the question of how one teaches and in the end; this activity will have a positive effect on the improvement of teaching (Hubbal, Collins, & Pratt, 2005, p. 60).

It is argued that reflection begins with one's perplexity about a topic and the willingness to adopt an attitude of suspended conclusion while studying the issue, gathering information, and gaining new knowledge. This reflection affords teachers conscious, deliberate insight to bring about enhanced student learning, and encourages teachers to become students of their own professional actions (Danielson, 2008, p. 130).

In a previous study (Wlodarsky & Walters, 2006), we observed that college faculty did demonstrate reflection, and this reflection manifested as cognitive processing of data from both internal sources (e.g., driving alone in a car and thinking about a class) and external sources (e.g., asking a peer for input). Additionally, this study identified the affective elements of self-judgment and evaluation as part of these faculty members' responses. The respondents "seemed concerned with finding value or judging the worth of their teaching" (p. 12). This reflection also was driven by an event, which was uniformly a classroom teaching experience, and was fundamentally evaluative in nature. This line of research raises concerns and questions related to theoretical models for reflection, and how relevant or accurate current models are for describing faculty performance. For example, Schön's (1983, 1987) model of reflection suggests that reflection on action must lead to change in the future, whereas King and Kitchner's (1994) model posits reflection developmentally and does not require change in future action. This difference highlights the need for clarity through new model development such as that undertaken in our research.

Critical reflection refers to an activity or process in which experience is recalled, considered, and evaluated, usually in relation to a broader purpose. Richards (1990) argued "it is a response to a past experience and involves conscious recall and examination of the experience as a basis for evaluation and decision making and as a source for planning and action" (p. 5).

As discussed in Mahnaz (1997), reflective thinking and teaching have also been defined as metacognition or self-monitoring based on cognitive-mediational theories of learning. Metacognition is "thinking about one's own thinking," and relates to this study of reflection as the researchers have attempted to operationalize the internal thought processes and external experiences which collectively become or contribute to "metacognition."

Freire (1993) discussed the concept of reflection as critically related to the cognitive difference between animals and humans and, as related to the process of humanization, as individuals evolve socially toward complete self-awareness from the stage of blind acceptance of reality, which he termed oppression. Reflection is an objectification of experience in time, "epochs of past, present, and future" (p. 83), that allows a human being to plan for a different future.

THE CENTRALITY OF REFLECTION

Reflection as a core practice remains a goal of education, especially higher education; this is evident in several recent national reports by the American Association of Colleges and Universities, American Association of Higher Education, American College Personnel Association, and National Association of Student Personnel Administrators, on undergraduate education, each of which reiterated the need for college graduates to think reflectively (as cited in King & Kitchener, 2004).

Among the most critical professional characteristics of teacher educators is that of reflectivity. The ability to self-judge our own practice context, capability, and performance against the broader professional contexts of practice by teacher educators has been noted by the National Council for Accreditation of Teacher Education (NCATE). The capacity for teacher educators to demonstrate professional reflection and to inculcate this capacity in prelicensure candidates in colleges of education is among the standards for accreditation in the NCATE criteria (NCATE, Standard 2). As a consequence, research designed to uncover this reflective capacity, to scale it for comparative study, and to relate it to standard measures of program quality are viewed as critical to a more realistic understanding of the capability of faculty in higher education (teacher educators) to meet the reform goals for K-12 education broadly.

PROFESSIONAL DEVELOPMENT MODELS AND REFLECTION

Unfortunately, traditional models of professional development for educators have been built from a cognition model in isolation from the increasingly complex practice environment, where decision making is clouded by conflicting policy and sociocultural constraints, although numerous calls to reform have been repeatedly issued. Butler (2004) noted a further deficiency with respect to professional development: "A related criticism of the traditional model is that it is based on questionable assumptions about the nature and origins of professional knowledge, and about how to forge connections between research and practice" (p. 437). In this gap, as has been noted frequently, what passes for educational development is typically disjointed, incoherent, and unconnected from authentic professional decision-making responsibilities for educators at all levels (Corcoran, 1995; Day, 1993; Livneh & Livneh, 1999).

STUDIES USING KING AND KITCHENER'S EPISTEMIC JUDGMENT MODEL

Research has consistently demonstrated a significant relationship between educational level and a person's ability to make reflective judgments. According to Friedman (2004), those with more formal education are more likely than those with less education to exhibit the most complex types of thinking described in King and Kitchener's reflective judgment model (RJM).

Although often compared with critical thinking, the RJM is distinct in its emphasis on the intellectual tasks involved in open-ended problem solving rather than closed-ended, the attention to epistemic assumptions, and the articulation of stages of development (Hofer, 2001).

Ill-defined problems, according to King and Kitchener (2004, p. 5) are characterized by two features: they cannot be defined with a high degree of completeness and they cannot be solved with a high degree of certainty.

After 25 years of investigating how late adolescents and adults come to understand and make judgments about kinds of controversial problems, three observations have been made by King and Kitchener: (a) there are striking differences in people's underlying assumptions about knowledge or epistemic assumptions, (b) these differences in assumptions are related to the way people make and justify their own judgments about ill structured problems, and, (c) there is a developmental sequence in the patterns of responses and judgments about such problems. The RJM provides a theoretical framework for understanding and organizing these observations (2004, p. 5).

King and Kitchener (2004) also observed that development in reasoning has stage-like properties, but not that it evolves in a lock step, one stage at a time fashion (p. 9). They delineate seven stages or levels of reflection that are organized into view of knowledge and concept of justification. The stages are as follows:

1. Knowledge is absolute, concrete with external authority and beliefs need no justification and no alternatives are perceived.
2. Knowledge is absolute but partial with external authority and existence of alternative views is acknowledged however, absolute knowledge is still maintained. There is a right way to believe.
3. Knowledge is absolute and uncertainty is temporary until external authority finds truth and beliefs are justified by reference to an authority's view.
4. Knowledge is uncertain and ambiguous and beliefs are justified by reasons and using evidence.
5. Knowledge is contextual and subjective and beliefs are justified within a particular context.
6. Knowledge is constructed from a variety of sources and beliefs are justified by comparing evidence and opinion across different contexts.
7. Knowledge is constructed through a process of inquiry and beliefs are justified probabilistically based on a variety of interpretive considerations (2004).

For example, it is common to find an individual who relies heavily on Stage 4 assumptions while reasoning about a controversial problem but who also makes statements that are consistent with Stage 3 and Stage 5 assumptions. By contrast, someone who relies heavily on Stage 2 assumptions rarely uses assumptions of any stage higher than Stage 3 of their seven stage process.

Additional researchers have used King and Kitchener's Reflective Judgment Model with a variety of populations. Dale (2005) completed a study in which the participants were students preparing for the ministry. The results of this study indicated that differences between entering and graduating students' Reflective Judgment Interview (RJI) mean scores were not statistically significant, nor were their mean scores significant between religious and secular dilemmas. Further, students' scores did not decrease significantly as their references to faith increased.

Friedman (2004) interviewed female students using the Omnibus Personality Inventory and the Reflective Judgment Interview and found that scores on six scales of the personality inventory correlated significantly with RJI scores; these include thinking introversion, response bias, altruism, autonomy, complexity, and theoretical orientation. These findings support the conclusion that post formal reasoning, as described by King and Kitchener's model, is related to measurable personality traits).

Ilacqua and Prescott (2003) used the reflective judgment model in their introductory economics courses and found that older students were more comfortable with uncertainty and complexity and more flexible in their interpretation of knowledge than the younger students.

Pirttila-Backmän and Kajanne (2001) published results that focused on Finnish adults. The RJM average stage score clearly increased during the two study periods; one initially given in the late 1980s and a follow up in the mid 1990s. Education, in particular, education beyond a person's primary profession/occupation was a strong predictor of development. Also, encountering diversity and exploratory orientation were related to development, but their connections were more complicated. No gender differences were found. The results support the idea that positive changes in thinking and reasoning take place during adulthood.

Pirttila-Backmän (1993) completed a Finnish cross-sectional study in which it was shown that both educational level (lower vocational, higher vocational and university) and field (technical, nursing/medical and social sciences) make a difference in the RJ scores. It was further shown that such factors as living in a complex environment, being responsible for other people and having autonomy in one's work seem to be related to the development of RJ. The lower one's education level, the more important are other life experiences (as cited in Pirttila-Backmän & Kajanne, 2001, p. 82).

REFLECTIVE CAPACITY AND PROFESSIONAL GROWTH

Among the most critical professional characteristics of teacher educators is that of reflectivity. A professor's capacity to reflect is directly related to her capacity to grow as a professional. The ability to self-judge our own practice context, capability, and performance against the broader professional contexts of practice by teacher educators has been noted by the NCATE. The capacity for teacher educators to demonstrate professional reflection and to inculcate this capacity in prelicensure candidates in colleges of education is among the standards for accreditation in the NCATE criteria (NCATE, Standard 2). As a consequence, research designed to uncover this reflective capacity, to scale it for comparative study, and to relate it to standard measures of program quality are viewed as critical to a more realistic understanding of the capability of college teachers in higher education (teacher educators) to meet the reform goals for K-12 education broadly. If we do not grow in our capacity for reflection, we will be limited in our capacity for professional growth.

Unfortunately, traditional models of professional development for educators have been built from a cognition model in isolation from the increasingly complex practice environment where decision making is clouded by conflicting policy and sociocultural constraints.

WLODARSKY AND WALTERS' REFLECTIVE CAPACITY STUDY

We applied the reflective practice scale developed by King and Kitchener (1994) to teacher educators in a college setting. Seeking to move from the narrow focus of their research problem as outlined above, we made several observations and were struck with a number of practical implications for colleges of education and their faculty (Wlodarsky & Walters, 2010).

First, facilitating and enhancing the capability of teacher educators to be reflective and to inculcate reflectivity among licensure candidates is critical to the success of the teaching profession. Consequently, identifying a reliable and valid conceptual model to operationalize and measure reflection among these groups is an important step to identifying practice solutions that are effective and sustainable. Incorporating the RJM in our study has been found to be appropriate and reliable, and to accommodate the cultural vocabulary of teacher educators.

The King and Kitchener stage model, when used as a rubric to scale teacher educator reflective capacity, was functional with a very high measured reliability. Were this type of scale used consistently with larger groups of teacher educators over time and in various demographic and sociocultural environments, important variables related to the formation of reflective capacity among teacher educators might be observed.

Further, given that the RJM proved reliable for scaling teacher educators' reflective capability, it would be appropriate to directly compare reflective scores for teacher educators to other professions which have been studied with this same RJM. In many areas of educational research, traditional research lines have failed to yield fruitful and energizing results which hold promise for powerful impact on the field of practice. Findings on research with other professional groups which used the RJM may contribute to a deeper understanding of reflection among teacher educators, thereby enhancing and facilitating growth in reflection and, subsequently, enhance reflective ability among their students, i.e. licensure candidates. These findings may also open new research lines toward an understanding of the relationship of self-awareness to professional competence for teacher educators, and how these translate to licensure candidates under the direction of these teacher educators. Finally, as noted in Chapter 1, disconnect between teacher educators and other on-campus colleagues might be addressed through these cross disciplinary comparison studies.

Second, we have clearly observed and cited the use of a common instrument and conceptual construct that functions reliably across a broad group of populations whose commonalities are adulthood, continuous learning beyond necessarily formal or institutional settings, and learning in professional contexts. This all-encompassing approach to literature has been a hallmark of the adult education movement in the United States since its inception and as an approach enriches our research and learning. The failure to incorporate the rich traditions and literatures across the fields engaged with adult learning has become an obstacle to professional renewal and growth in our field, that of teacher education. Within our own college setting, the insularity that is produced through overlimitation of literary categories, through overreliance on literature specific to teacher educators, and through an unnecessary delimiting of learning from multiple fields of inquiry, is at the very least intellectually stifling.

Pragmatically, there is much we can learn about ourselves as teacher educators if we learn to first view ourselves as adult learners generally, with much in common with individuals and colleagues from many other traditions and contexts. We may find solutions to what we have construed as unique practice problems to teacher education from those other traditions.

Third, in our study, every participant revealed narrative from every level of the RJM. However, a clear preponderance of scores revealed an average or typical reflective level of slightly higher than 4.0 (see numbered descriptions for scale scores). This observation supports King and Kitchener's findings, which observed that individuals would have a typical level, while occasionally responding above or below that level. However, we were surprised to observe that typical, cultural characterizations of teacher educators, i.e. highly postmodernist and constructivist in orientation, did not hold up in this analysis. Teacher educators were more typically found to be at the center of the epistemic scale. They were comfortable with authoritative knowledge, external authority and evidence, and objectivity and rationalism as the means to understanding. This finding would situate the field of teacher education more centrally and philosophically than modern social preconceptions held by the general public.

Given the relatively midrange of scores of the college teachers we studied and our perception that they are not atypical of college teachers in other institutions, there is room for professional development to enhance the evolution of college teachers with respect to personal reflective capacity. There was a gap observed in the response scores of college teachers in our study and those obtained by Glenn and Eklund (1991) in their study of late career college teachers members. To the degree that our participants are similar to the college teachers studied by Glenn and Eklund, it is important to identify the types of professional development that mid- to late-career professors might engage in that would result in the kind of growth in reflective judgment required to move from the approximately 4.0 stage to the high 5.0 stage. For our college teachers, it may be possible to develop a trajectory of growth in reflective capacity on the King and Kitchener scale based on their current levels, the professional growth activities in which they engage, and their similarity or difference to the Glenn and Eklund study sample. Our research and the literary context we've established suggests that structured, formal learning generally associated with classical, liberal arts, or content in nature would contribute to increasing the reflective capacity of college teachers. More broadly construed, and noting that the following thought is perhaps fodder for an entirely different and lengthy conversation (as discussed in Chapter 1), the ongoing concerns over the preparation or fit of teacher educators within the academy may also be ameliorated. Of great potential here is the use of increased formal learning experiences to broaden and deepen the content knowledge of these individuals, which might also contribute to the creation of more reflective college teachers generally.

REFLECTION AND ADULT DEVELOPMENT

Reflective judgment also appears to be related to other dimensions of development. King and Shuford (1996) found a moderate positive relationship between the kinds of assumptions students use to reason about intellectual issues and the assumptions they use to reason about moral issues. Guthrie, King, and Palmer found moderate positive correlations between reflective thinking and tolerance for diversity (1999, as cited in King & Kitchener, 2004, p. 22). Participants in this study who reasoned at quasi and reflective thinking levels were much more likely to hold tolerant viewpoints with respect to race and sexual orientation than their counterparts who help prereflective assumptions.

The strongest contrast between college-educated and noncollege educated adults is provided by Glenn and Eklund (1991, as cited in King & Kitchener, 1994, pp. 174). These researchers administered the RJI to two groups of participants who were at least 65 years old but who differed in terms of their educational attainment. The first group consisted of adults with up to a high school education: their RJI mean score was 3.7, which is about half a stage higher than the overall mean score among high school seniors (3.3) and closer to the average for the college samples (3.8). The second group consisted of retired faculty members with doctorates; the RJI mean score for this group was 5.2, which is comparable to the scores earned by advanced graduate students.

COGNITIVE GROWTH AND REFLECTION

The connection between cognition and reflection was described by King (1992, 2000) and King and Kitchener (1994, 2004) as the development of *reflective judgment* or *epistemic cognition*. These terms are defined as "a developmental progression that occurs between childhood and adulthood in the way people understand the process of knowing and in the corresponding ways that they justify their beliefs about ill-structured problems" (King & Kitchener, 1994, p. 13). This cognition-reflection model has been validated in studies with nurses (Platzer, Drake, & Ashford, 2000a, 2000b); preservice education majors (Amobi, 2003); economics majors in BS degree programs (Ilacqua & Prescott, 2003); with female students (Friedman, 2004); with seminary students (Dale, 2005); with both young and middle-years adults (Pirttila-Backman & Kajanne, 2001), and with lay-adults in Finland (Kajanne, 2003). Pascarella and Terenzini (2005) suggested that the King and Kitchener model may be the "best known and most extensively studied" cognitive growth model. However, we have failed to find a study where the model had been applied to the ill-structured problems inherent in the professional practices of higher education faculty members.

King and Kitchener (1994, 2004) suggested that the emergence of both cognition and reflective capacity in adulthood is developmental, a stage theory. These stages are viewed as both optimal (the upper limits of capability) and functional (the typical level of operation), and adults frequently apply cognitive strategies or epistemologies from more than one stage to any given problem-solving scenario. Of interest to our research is the movement from personal cognition in problem solving (King & Kitchener's Stages 1 through 3) toward a social cognition of problem solving (Stages 4 and 5) wherein the individual is capable of allowing others access to the reflection and cognition process. We detected this phenomenon in many participants in our research where they identify the role of a trusted peer in critical reflection on performance, and we pursue this concept later in this text. More specifically to this current section, is the observation at the higher stages, that is Stage 6 and Stage 7, that "complex problems require some type of thinking action before a resolution can be constructed" (King & Kitchener, 1994, p. 67). Hence, when we capture the terms *thinking, thinking about, examine* or *focused thinking* in participant narratives, we are most likely observing higher level reflection by the participants under the King and Kitchener model.

Dewey (1933) and Schön (1983) argued for a proactive and learner-centered form of reflection in which the practitioner becomes the owner of, and subject in, the process of his or her own reflection. This will result in developing a language for talking and thinking about their own practices, questioning the sometimes contradictory beliefs underpinning their practice, and taking greater control over their own professional growth. For more details regarding cognition as it relates to reflection, see Chapter 6.

RECOMMENDATIONS FOR PRACTICE

Where does the individual professor or college go in response to such a thick summation of the historic and literary background of the construct *reflection*? We believe that individual professors and colleges should take the time to intentionally work through their own definition of reflection and how that definition is observed in and around their practice behaviors as professionals.

QUESTIONS FOR INDIVIDUAL FOLLOW-UP

1. How do you define reflection?
2. Do you consider reflection to be an intentional process that should be included periodically in your evolving analysis of your contributions as a faculty member?
3. Are there discrete steps involved with your reflective actions?
4. Is reflection, for you as an individual, an amorphous or implied behavior, or can you point to discrete tasks that you take to be reflective?
5. How do you link reflection, if you view it as a discrete activity, to your broader activities as a professor and scholar?
6. How does your department or college require you to demonstrate reflection in annual reports or portfolios in some way? And if so, how is the term or activity operationalized for you?

QUESTIONS FOR GROUP OR ORGANIZATIONAL CONSIDERATION

1. Does the college use the term *reflection* in any way as a description of its core values or behaviors, or should it?
2. If it uses the idea, what is the context, real or implied, in the use of the term? For example, do you make the statement "We are a

reflective college"? If so, what does that really mean to the organization? Describe the times and institutional personnel who are tasked with being reflective in some way?

3. At a college meeting, review college documents that state or imply that your organization is reflective. Can the faculty clearly, and with agreement, define the meaning of the term? How can the practice of reflection be described from college practices? Can the faculty develop a list of evidences that the organization is, in fact, reflective if it makes that claim?

4. If the college claims to be reflective, where, when, how, and who is involved in this task or process? Is it a committee assignment? Is it a "buzz word" that sounds intensely important? Or is it more than this?

As the individual professor or college faculty as a group works through the process of more carefully defining the meaning of reflection and how he or she or they use the term, it is likely that the individual and the college as a whole will walk through some of the same emotional responses as our Dr. Kathy Burton did in the story at the beginning of this chapter. So busy in the daily grind of the job, she had, by late in the year, failed, in her mind, to juggle the competing demands of the college in which she was working.

CHAPTER 3

CHARACTERISTICS OF REFLECTION AMONG COLLEGE TEACHERS

When Joseph started college, he didn't imagine himself in the role of a college teacher when he envisioned his future. He felt like just one of many people in the system, trying to complete his degree, to make something of himself. Hoping someone would give him a chance in the workforce, so he could make money to pay the bills.

Something nagged at him about his undergraduate education; something was missing. He felt that he was simply supposed to "go through the motions" to complete his degree; like jumping through a hoop. None of his teachers were asking much of him; they didn't challenge him, ask him to think, question, to reflect. He spent hours thinking about his college classroom experiences. From a student perspective, what was working for him? What wasn't working for him? He made a conscious choice to internalize his experiences and analyze them, searching for reasonable explanations; how could he fix his situation? It was a void for Joseph, one that would become the catalyst for defining his career path.

His investigation evolved into a research agenda that has spanned his career as a college teacher with the goal of better understanding reflection, encouraging college teachers to be reflective, and providing an effective process to do so.

Joseph's feelings intensified regarding the "lack of thinking" in the classroom by teachers and students. He spent time picking the brains of his closest friends—several of his current classmates—wanting to know if they felt the same way. Did his classmates think there was a void in their education? Did they feel as if they

Reflection and the College Teacher: A Solution for Higher Education
pp. 33–43
Copyright © 2014 by Information Age Publishing
All rights of reproduction in any form reserved.

were being asked to think, to question, to reflect? He wanted input from his peers regarding experiences he defined as problematic.

As a college student for years, he knew somewhat what it meant to reflect. It certainly made him feel vulnerable, willing to admit there may be problem(s); becoming willing to admit that he might not know the "answer"; or admitting that he didn't know, really, what it means to reflect and/or how to reflect. As Joseph thought about this, he realized there was an evaluative nature to reflection that created a level of discomfort in students and teachers within the classroom. This evaluative aspect of reflection could certainly have an influence as to whether or not individuals chose to reflect and if so, how authentic the reflection was.

CENTRAL ISSUE OF THE CHAPTER

We have deduced definitions of reflection out of the historical literature; this is important to our overall understanding of reflection, however, it is as important to clarify the essential characteristics of reflection as practiced by college teachers. Wlodarsky (2005) found that reflection among college teachers could be linked to changed beliefs and practices in their classrooms. In this chapter, we describe the nature and characteristics of reflective practice in an authentic setting, connecting theory to practice.

Our research described the nature and characteristics of reflective practice and the associative strength of these characteristics with select demographic variables identified in the literature, and collected by the researchers for their study population. An initial analysis of the data indicated that reflection for the participants was an internal, cognitive process using the brain as the primary *tool*. Second, it was evident that the participants were open to input from their peer(s); those they specifically defined as confidants. It appeared that this informal setting provided a comfort level in which the participants were open to positive and negative feedback. Third, reflection was fundamentally driven by an evaluative, judgmental frame of reference. These participants seemed concerned with finding value or judging the worth of their teaching. Finally, the brief definition of *reflection* defined by the majority of the participants referenced their beliefs and practices about their teaching; they didn't focus on research or service. Figure 3.1 represents conceptual clusters of reflection from our study that frames this chapter and many of the following chapters (Wlodarsky & Walters' 2006).

REFLECTION AS AN INTERNAL COGNITIVE PROCESS

I would describe reflection as an act of processing what happened on a particular day with a particular lesson; a deconstruction. Reflection is focused thinking that facilitates deeper exploration and contextual meaning from

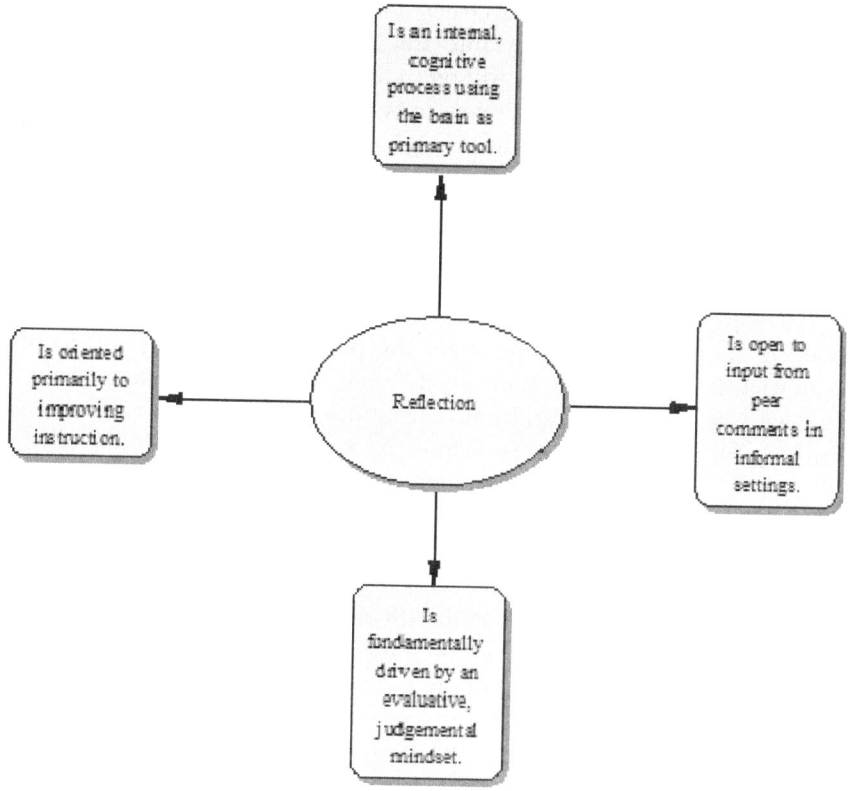

Figure 3.1.   Conceptual clusters of reflection.

an experience. The goal of reflection is to build on the things that worked and rethink the aspects that didn't. I often use my commute to critically examine why something was successful and what may have impacted the successes and failures. (Dr. CC, select quote from research participant)

Reflection can be viewed as an internal, cognitive process using the brain as the primary tool. External planning documents, formalized data collection or analysis, or journals are not typically incorporated to assist reflection or to help college teachers overcome personal biases which may have been overly critical. The tendency rather is to evaluate beliefs and practices using cognition as a means to an end; the goal is to improve practices deemed unsuccessful, or weak; engaging in a cognitive process whereby an awareness surfaces, a sense of knowing emerges. In short, college teachers have to "think about" their experiences for some period of time. The reflective process is clearly localized, personal, and cognitive and we will dig more deeply into this cognitive aspect in Chapter 6. Although college teachers are willing to listen to input from their peers, a significant part of the process tends to be private, a process which no one else knows about unless the individual decides to reveal it, the hidden thoughts of the college teachers (Wlodarsky &Walters, 2006).

The connection between cognition and reflection was described by King (1992, 2000) and King and Kitchener (1994, 2004) as the development of *reflective judgment* or *epistemic cognition*. These terms are defined as "a developmental progression that occurs between childhood and adulthood in the way people understand the process of knowing and in the corresponding ways that they justify their beliefs about ill-structured problems (p. 13). This cognition-reflection model has been validated in studies with teacher educators (Wlodarsky & Walters, 2006, 2010), nurses (Platzer, Brake, & Ashford, 2000a, 2000b); preservice education majors (Amobi, 2003); economics majors in BS degree programs (Ilacqua & Prescott, 2003); with female students (Friedman, 2004); with seminary students (Dale, 2005); with both young and middle-years adults (Pirttila-Backman & Kajanne, 2001), and with lay-adults in Finland (Kajanne, 2003). Pascarella and Terenzini (2005) suggested that the King and Kitchener model may be the "best known and most extensively studied" cognitive growth model.

King and Kitchener (1994, 2004) suggested that the emergence of both cognition and reflective capacity in adulthood is a developmental stage theory. These stages are viewed as both optimal (the upper limits of capability) and functional (the typical level of operation), and adults frequently apply cognitive strategies or epistemologies from more than one stage to any given problem-solving scenario.

We were interested in the movement from personal cognition in problem solving (King and Kitchener's Stages 1 through 3) toward a social cognition of problem solving (Stages 4 and 5) wherein the individual is capable of allowing "others" access to the reflection and cognition process. In this study, we detected this phenomena in many of the college teachers we studied that college teachers identified the role of a trusted peer in critical reflection on performance. More specifically is the observation at King and Kitchener's Stages, 6 and 7, that "complex problems require some type of thinking action before a resolution can be constructed" (1994, p. 67). Hence, when we captured the terms *thinking*, *thinking about, examine* or *focused thinking* in participant narratives, we were most likely observing higher level reflection by the participants as described by King and Kitchener's model.

REFLECTIVE PROCESS CONSISTS OF PEER INPUT

College teachers are open to input from their peer(s); those they specifically defined as confidants. This process of feedback or input tends to take place in informal settings, that is, in the hallway, one's office or at lunch. Informal settings can provided a comfort level in which individuals are open to positive and negative feedback. The informal setting tends to make individuals feel less vulnerable, and in turn, more willing to allow for input. This part of the reflective process still can be defined as internal. Individuals are still choosing to process information; however, the actual information being processed comes from an external source (Wlodarsky & Walters, 2006). In her annual review, Dr. PE talks at length about the importance of peer input,

> For the past 3 years, as a part of my team teaching experiment with a colleague, she and I have engaged in weekly and sometimes daily discussions about how we can improve our instruction of methods for undergraduates and at the same time model team processes, cooperative learning and the value of diversity of thought in a complex endeavor. I have found this relationship with my colleague and mentor incredibly helpful for instructional refinement. My student's evaluations have improved, and my satisfaction with the quality of our instruction has increased.

Another college teacher, Dr. JK, spoke about the reflective process,

> I openly talk with colleagues about teaching situations that I do not feel were as successful as they should have been. This might be based on student evaluations or my sense of student performance or attitude. I keep in close communication with colleagues regarding the content of courses. I ponder about how each class went at the end of every day. If something did not go well, I dwell on it for days and usually have to discuss it with someone.

Input from peers in an informal setting can be considered a "mentoring" experience. Weasmer and Woods (2003) found that teachers identified reflection as a primary outcome of the mentoring experience. They found that mentoring a student teacher motivated participants to rely upon reflection-on-action to validate or to reframe thinking and consider modifying practice. As the students, ripe with awareness of contemporary pedagogy, shared the classroom, learning was reciprocal. Also, because teaching is usually an isolated activity, the added presence of a student teacher in most cases resulted in a pleasant collegial environment (p.68)

Data from a study completed by Burbank and Kauchak (2003) indicated that collaborative action research was perceived positively by both preservice and in-service teachers on a number of dimensions including

changing teaching practice, changing views about research and as a vehi-
cle to dialogue about research and teaching practice. This finding was
especially robust for the experienced teachers participating in collaboration. In addition, teaming led to feelings of community and professionalism.

In a study completed by Hatala (2002), she argued that the simple fact
that professors agreed to participate in the study was an indication that
they thought reflecting on one's beliefs and practices was important. The
participants were aware that the researcher would be asking them to think
about student learning and teaching and its relationship to practice. The
presence of the researcher throughout the observations, as commented by
all the participants, provided an awareness of what was taking place
within the classroom context that had not existed before. In addition, the
dialogue between the researcher and participant(s) after class observations allowed for reflection of their beliefs and practices. Last, the focus
group discussions that took place throughout the study provided a means
for issues to surface pertaining to student learning and teaching. Simply
allowing oneself to listen and respond to others facilitated self-reflection.
Participants of the study interacted as *peers* and also to some extent, the
researcher conceptually served as a *peer*.

Hatala (2002) observed different types of reflection were taking place;
for example, there was private reflection during the survey and interviews
and social reflection during the after-class reflections and focus groups.
According to Hatala, this distinction was significant in that social reflection seemed to be more influential in terms of awareness and behavior
change than did private reflection. The themes of mentoring, collegial
relationships and professional dialogue account for the importance of this
type of reflection in creating awareness and behavior change in college
classrooms.

Quinlan and Akerlind's (2000) study demonstrated the importance of
considering the context within which peer review of innovative teaching
and collaborative teaching activities are attempted. The discipline, the
college, and the department all contribute to shaping the context and
appropriate nature of such innovations. Based on current research, college teachers will most likely react positively to collaboration if: (a) collaborative work patterns already exist, (b) agreement exists upon a set of
external standards, (c) an involvement in education reform is present, (d)
the college teachers' desire for the need or problem to be addressed, (e)
reasonable levels of morale and trust are present, and (f) confidence is
there in terms of status and reputation.

Looking at the reflection model proposed by King and Kitchener
(1994), the movement from personal, internal reflective thought relying
on an epistemology that is closed to external interpretation of evidence

toward reflective thought that is open to ambiguity, to questioning of self-interpretation, and to greater openness and reliance on social reflection via peer and confidant communications, would be considered evidence of growth in reflective complexity. Some college teachers begin with private contemplation of professional activity, such as while driving alone in a car after class, only to later approach a colleague for input. This observation supports King and Kitchener's contention that multiple stages of reflection will be incorporated around the same proximate event.

THE EVALUATIVE NATURE OF REFLECTION

Can the reflective process be detached from evaluation, or judgment? We believe the answer is *no*. Reflection is fundamentally driven by an evaluative, judgmental or critical frame of reference. College teachers seem concerned with finding value or judging the worth of their teaching. College teachers tend to assign a value system to their reflections, that is, clearly focusing on weaknesses in teaching and then engaging in a thought process that would ultimately improve their teaching practices.

Dr. CE defined reflection, "thinking in an evaluative way about one's practice and making a plan to improve." This college teacher mentioned the tools she uses to reflect. These included student products, student evaluations, peer evaluations of teaching, feedback from annual reviews and the promotion and tenure process." Dr. JK appears to agree with Dr. CE, as she connects reflection to the evaluative process of the institution. Dr. JK commented,

I spend considerable time on my annual evaluations as I think and write comments about each course. I am not good at accepting criticism and often I have to have time to consider my weaknesses and failures. I am fortunate to have a department chair who sees his role as one of support and not of finding fault. I think when, in the past, I had a chair who always sought to identify weaknesses that I was not as forth coming with those problems. Now I feel confident in presenting the positive and negative about my performance during chair evaluations. I do think reflection depends somewhat on the ultimate audience, whether private or public. I am still cautious about what I write and the written product doesn't really reveal my level of reflection. I see the written evaluation more as a reminder of what I want to discuss. I tell my chair about problems at a more in-depth level than I write.

King and Kitchener (2004) discussed the relationship of personal epistemologies, proofs for knowledge, and the movement away from personal, unsubstantiated opinion toward evidence-based cognition and reflection. Underlying this continuum was an implicit movement in the developmental complexity of the individual away from a nonquestioning, cognitively simplistic belief, an absolute faith in personal knowledge. Across King and Kitcheners' stages, this belief system was gradually replaced by a cognitively complex, judgmental and critically reflective system of thought. There is an increased capability and proclivity to critique and judge one's performance and tentative solutions to ill-structured problems. King and Kitchener's model would explain our observation of the highly evaluative and critical frame of reference of many of the college teachers in our study. In fact, to the degree that King and Kitchener might be describing adult development generally they seem to predict that higher stages of reflection would manifest themselves with or through evaluative terminology.

REFLECTIVE PROCESS GRAVITATES TOWARD TEACHING

When I was asked to respond to the question, "what are the components of outstanding and inspiring teaching," I responded initially by saying, "Whew! That's a question that has occupied some of the world's greatest scholars for centuries. Although it is tempting to quote the greats, I want to take on the daunting task of distilling 35 years of my experience in education into a short list of what has seemed to work very effectively for me and most importantly, for my students.

On my short list of outstanding and inspiring teaching components, I included reflection. I believe in the importance of reflection, in particular, reflection on ones' teaching. The outstanding teacher will always analyze the data from the perspective of self-improvement. I feel very strongly that the difference between an average teacher and an outstanding one shows up most clearly when the data reveal a problem. The average teacher will say "Why didn't the kids try harder?", while the outstanding educator will reflectively ask "I wonder how I can teach this better?", and then make appropriate changes the next time the course in taught. (Dr. HB, select quote from research participant)

Reflection is the process I use to consider and reconsider my teaching methodology and its effects on student performance. It involves examining and reexamining my instruction, the projects I ask students to do, the problems I ask them to solve, their performance on assessment instruments and their reaction to my teaching performance with an eye to improving both the student's experience and outcome. (Dr. PE, select quote from research participant)

Although there are varying reasons for concern regarding the need for greater quality in college teaching, one thing is certain, the concern itself. Cross suggested that college teachers become classroom researchers

(1981, cited in Paulsen & Feldman, 1995). These college teachers would view their classrooms as laboratories where they could continually collect information about what and how their students learn in relation to what and how they are being taught. Through careful reflection, instructors could establish meaningful connections between their own teaching behaviors and their students' learning processes and outcomes. Such efforts would also illuminate the content-specific characteristics of effective teaching in a particular discipline.

The involvement of teachers in searching for new knowledge about teaching effectiveness also begins to build a foundation for improved evaluation of teaching, an essential ingredient in rewarding teaching in promotion and tenure decisions. Cross stated (as cited in Paulsen & Feldman, 1995)

> I can think of no action that would do quite as much for the improvement of teaching and learning as to let a thousand classroom laboratories bloom across the nation. That would be taking teaching seriously, and it would move us toward our goal of quality education for all. (p. 14)

We found in our research that the majority of participants, when asked to discuss reflection, referenced their teaching; they did not focus on research or service, which should be significant components to their professional development, as well as their potential promotion and tenure.

CONCLUSION

Reflection has cognitive implications and limitations. Clearly, more work in this area would have both theoretical importance and practical importance for the development of instructional materials and resources in the cognitive domain to assist in the development of both reflective college teachers and K-12 teachers.

The notion of an informal mentoring experience among college teachers within higher education is important. College teachers are open to input from their peer(s); those they specifically defined as confidants. It would seem appropriate to explore the current literature on mentoring to determine additional characteristics and/or situations that would facilitate mentoring processes, in turn, allowing for college teachers to develop professionally using a team approach to reflection.

There is a link between reflection and personal improvement in somewhat of an evaluative frame of reference. College teachers refer to movement from weakness to strength and from failure to success. The use of the terms *evaluation*, *evaluate*, *judge*, and *assess* suggests a deficiency model when reflecting on one's teaching. This deficiency model is maintained when controlled for rank and tenure, that is, full, tenured professors demonstrate this deficiency mindset as well as junior college teachers. This deficiency or evaluative model of reflection should be explored further, as it has implications for posttenure college teachers' development and generalized motivation for reflection.

Improving the quality of higher education teaching is a task which has risen to national prominence, as evidenced by recent publications on quality issues in higher education (Levine, 2005; McNaught, 2003; Shuster, 2003). Nevertheless, our research finds a singular focus among study participants on the quality of their teaching which suggests that Levine's uniform criticisms are at least overgeneralized. Among college teachers there are individuals who maintain equity between research interests and teaching students. Whether or not this finding represents a cultural artifact of only the college teachers participating in Wlodarsky and Walters' study (2006) and/or this specific university environment, or whether this interest in improving teaching in higher education is a characteristic of a larger population of professors should be the subject of more careful and extensive research.

RECOMMENDATIONS FOR PRACTICE

Given a perspective on reflection that includes these four characteristics (internal cognitive process, peer input, evaluative nature, and related to teaching), it may be helpful for individual college teachers and colleges as a whole to consider the following questions.

QUESTIONS FOR INDIVIDUAL FOLLOW-UP

1. How did I use data to bracket and reveal my professional blind spots?
2. Do I solicit peer input to the various elements of my professional life?
3. How do I use the input I receive from my peers?
4. What does the evaluative process look like for your position as a college teacher?
5. Does the evaluative aspect of your position affect your desire and/or ability to reflect? If so, how?

QUESTIONS FOR GROUP OR ORGANIZATIONAL CONSIDERATION

1. Does the college have a requirement of reflection on teaching, research and service? If so, to what extent do these reflections affect the evaluation process?

2. To what extent has the college encouraged reflection, aside from the evaluation process?

3. Does the college offer support for reflection, that is, introducing the concept, or providing training in how to reflect?

4. How does the college define reflection?

5. Does the college encourage and/or require peer input to the various elements of my professional life? If so, to what extent is the peer input weighted?

CHAPTER 4

WHAT DOES THE REFLECTIVE PROCESS LOOK LIKE?

After losing her middle school teaching job due to budget cuts several years ago, Cathleen Sensitive was forced to take a job as a manager for a local department store. Several years into it, discouraged with the dead-end job, Cathleen, at 45 years of age, decided to quit her job and return to school to complete her doctorate. She realized soon into the program that she was quite successful as a doctoral student; she seemed to do well with the curriculum, even joking with her peers that she was textbook savvy and that is what it took to "get through the program." Cathleen graduated from her doctoral program and immediately accepted a faculty position at a small Midwestern college teaching primarily undergraduate students in the area of literacy. She felt quite confident going into the position, sensing that good teaching was the primary criteria for tenure. Cathleen thought to herself, "well, I've taught students before and I know my content well, this will be a piece of cake!"

Dr. Sensitive was feeling a sense of dread as she entered her office; she opened the envelope holding her student semester evaluation report. Tears flowed as she realized her evaluations were far from excellent. The majority of her students rated her as a poor instructor. She read through the detailed student comments realizing they were pervasively negative. Students made comments such as, "instructor doesn't know how to interact well with college students, she doesn't relate to the life and issues of a struggling college student." Another student said, "Her assignments don't make sense, I don't understand why she makes us complete activities that have nothing to do with the content." Yet another student complained that his roommate took this same course from Dr. Sensitive's 3 years ago, and nothing had

Reflection and the College Teacher: A Solution for Higher Education
pp. 45–55

changed. The course was exactly the same!" Dr. Sensitive realized, after reading through her evaluations, that teaching wasn't a "piece of cake" and her evaluations were the catalyst for change.

One of the values and student learner outcomes within Dr. Sensitive's college is reflection. She recalls reading the college brochure, as it stated, "Within the college of education, reflection is used as a tool to find stability in the midst of change. Faculty demonstrate reflection by identifying professional strengths and needs and by planning for professional growth to improve future performance." Dr. Sensitive wondered, "what does reflection actually look like? And for that matter, is there an actual process that can be laid out or described?" Because she values teaching and wants her students to learn, and be productive in her courses, Dr. Sensitive decides to search for the answers to her questions, with the hope of eventually working through a reflective practice that ultimately improves her teaching, in turn, her students learn.

CHARACTERISTICS EVIDENT IN OTHER REFLECTIVE PROCESSES

This chapter introduces the Wlodarsky-Walters Event Path as a model which individuals and organizations can use for the reflective process. Our research has raised concerns and questions for us related to the theoretical models for reflection in past and contemporary literature, and how relevant or accurate or sufficiently nuanced these models are for describing reflective behaviors and processes of college faculty. Namely, most of these models, as is true of much in the field of education broadly, are highly skewed to outcomes thinking: what are the results, how do teachers change, what was different during the next cycle. For the models which more thickly describe reflection as a process or pathway, much attention is devoted to cognition and preparation for cognition via background knowledge and the individual's development, stage and/or phase of life and practice.

In a previous study (Wlodarsky & Walters, 2006), we observed that college faculty demonstrated reflection, and this reflection manifested as cognitive processing of data from both internal sources (e.g., driving alone in a car and thinking about a class) and external sources (e.g., asking a peer for input). Additionally, the respondents "seemed concerned with finding value or judging the worth of their teaching" (p. 12). This reflection also was driven by an event, which was uniformly a classroom teaching experience, and was fundamentally evaluative in nature. This line of research raises concerns and questions related to theoretical models for reflection, and how relevant or accurate current models are for describing faculty performance.

Schön's (1983, 1987) model of reflection suggests that reflection on action must lead to change in the future, whereas King and Kitchner's (1994) model posits reflection developmentally and does not require change in future action. This difference highlights the need for clarity through new model development such as that undertaken in our research.

More recently, Sen and Ford (2009) developed a model for reflection known as the SEA-change model. This model emphasized the importance of past and present experiences and possible future developments. It confirmed the importance of situation or context in the reflective process. The reflection draws on evidence often from experience or research, from which learning takes place and culminates in the identification of the need for change. The model has three core process elements: a consideration of the situation (S); consideration of the evidence used during the practice of reflection (E); and action (A) needed as a result of what has been learned from the reflective process. Sen and Ford discuss reflection in relation to teachers or mentors applying a progressive "de-scaffolding" approach to learning support in order to facilitate student autonomy (pp. 193-194).

Kahn et al. (2008, p. 165) reviewed the literature on coherent theoretically based approaches to the use of reflective processes. Their work resulted in a framework that allows us to realize elements that may be emphasized in a reflective process. A core reflective process emphasizes the *task*—an extended activity or set of activity and *focus*—the aspect of, or foundations for, practice investigated during the task. Other reflective processes tend to focus on the *social interactions* between participants, facilitators and others which may help sustain the process. For some models, *personal biases*, factors influencing how an individual engages in a reflective process, are underscored. The importance of considering the *wider context* in the reflective process is mentioned in some models. In other cases, the emphasis is placed on the *theoretical basis*—foundations for the reflective process. Last, as mentioned previously, *outcomes*, resulting from following a reflective process, is the primary element.

We accept the importance of continuous improvement and professional change, as well as cognition and professional preparation and development as such models helped us refine our model. However, it should be noted that although the existing literature describing the reflective process was helpful, it was still lacking in practical connections and coherent language and, thus, warranted additional exploration.

INTRODUCTION TO THE STUDY

As part of our research, we recruited a voluntary sample of professors within a college of education at a private, liberal arts university in the Midwest. This college uses a reflection-based model of annual faculty review and professional development. As part of the data collection, respondents defined reflection and discussed select tools or cognitive processes, which they used to facilitate reflection on their own professional development. We used a qualitative coding strategy to examine the process(es) described in the participant responses. We worked independently of each other to establish initial themes and categories among the narrative responses as a first step in enhancing the credibility of the project. The themes which emerged have been observed in related literature as cited throughout this chapter, and the remainder of the book providing additional confirmatory support for the reliability and credibility of these emerging themes.

We used the respondents' terms to organize the narrative, employing an analytic concept mapping procedure described by Novak (1998) and Novak and Gowen (1984). This procedure allowed us to both organize and label participant responses. We coded the first participant's survey responses together to standardize the coding process. Following agreement on the process to be used, we separately coded two additional responses, and then compared their respective maps to monitor agreement on the process and consistency of coding. We then individually coded the remaining responses, creating a total of 17 concept maps.

WLODARSKY-WALTERS EVENT PATH

This model is an elegant approach for analyzing the professional reflections of college faculty members. The terminology supplied by the respondents in the survey narrative are indicators of individual cognitive, epistemological, developmental, and reflective levels or stages. Furthermore, affective elements such as satisfaction, and confidence or the lack thereof, were threaded through and not distinguishable from these other dimensions of human development and self-evaluation.   Consequently, this model provides an organizing framework, which may be useful for planning professional development for faculty members.

The event path that we described answers our original research question: what might reflection actually look like? Fourteen of the 17 concept maps had strong similarities. This implies that a preponderance of participants use the same reflective process to consider their own professional activities. The meta-map depicts the typical path followed by the respondents (Figure 4.1) and is consistent with the 14 maps developed around the respondents' narratives.

This figure indicates a precipitating *Event*, followed by an intentional period of *Cognitive* processing of information. The *Cognition* component serves as the point in which the problem is formulated. The information

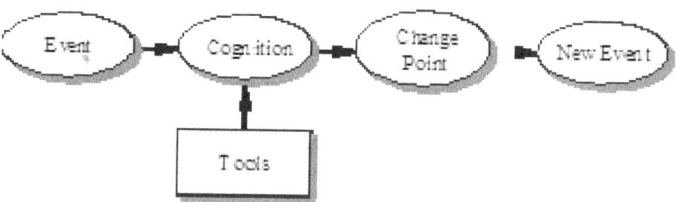

Figure 4.1.   Event path for professional reflection.

processed during this cognitive period is derived from *Tools,* which vary from individual to individual, although the discussion below briefly notes the common clusters of tools used by these respondents. The researchers view the *Tools* component of the path as a form of data collection by the respondents. For 14 of the respondents, these phenomena are followed by a *Change Point,* where a decision or judgment is made about future behavior. This *New Event* terminology is not delineated separately in the discussion below as it included the same terminology found in the *Event* narrative. For three of the respondents, there was not a clear indication that a new event emerged.

The discussion section describes the narrative provided by the respondents associated with each of the segments on the *Event Path,* with implications from a broader literature review. Specific narratives are included in the sections that describe each of the components of the event path. It is believed that this model is an excellent approach for analyzing the professional reflections of college faculty members, and that the terminology supplied by the respondents in the survey narrative can be viewed as indicators of individual cognitive, epistemological (see Chapter 6), developmental, and reflective levels or stages (see Chapter 2). Furthermore, it was clear from the response language that affective elements such as satisfaction, and confidence or the lack thereof, were threaded through and not distinguishable from these other dimensions of human development and self-evaluation.

Discussion of Event Terminology

The importance of the *event* as the phenomenological trigger for reflection leading to change in professional practice cannot be overstated. This is the conceptual bedrock that allows a discussion of learning in or through practice, as opposed to learning about practice in a depersonalized manner. This type of thought was termed *technical rationality* by Schön (1983, 1987), whose now seminal works are the basis for much of contemporary thought on reflection. For Schön, the professional must expand upon technical understandings of the field of practice by an elaboration of experience through reflection-on, reflection-in and reflection-for authentic practice experiences. Reflection-on-action occurs after the action has been completed and is a look back on experience to better understand it. Reflection-in-action occurs during unique situations requiring problem solving in the midst of the experience. Reflection-for-action occurs when the individual begins to anticipate situations before being faced with them and/or begins to plan for the future to improve the present situation/outcome.

Campoy (2000) expanded the idea of the event using the term *opportunity*. The *opportunity* is an integral step in reflection. As such, professional development must be linked to authentic experiences. This allows individuals to move from lower level, descriptive, or scientific/definitional "retellings" toward more truly reflective, future-oriented understandings of practice.

This notion of the *event*, or Campoy's opportunity, is sustained and greatly expanded by King and Kitchner (2004) in their earliest (Stages 1 and 2) levels of reflective practice. For professionals at these levels, there is "an assumption that knowledge is gained through direct personal *observations*" (p. 7) (i.e., direct personal experience). This language is consistent with Campoy (2000) and Schön (1987), and is also consistent with our identification of the practice event. Thus, our label event is conceptually identical to Campoy's *opportunity*, King and Kitchner's observation and Schön's *professional action*. The observation of a similar underlying phenomenon for each of these terms across each of these lines of research enhances the credibility of these earlier studies as well as this current research.

For our participants, their process of professional development as college faculty began with an incident, an event of practice. This may have been a class session or a set of classes over a semester period. One participant specifically mentioned, "Looking back on lessons, presentations, and other pieces of work as a stimulus for reflection." Yet another stated, "The act of processing what happened on a particular day with a particular lesson; what made it an effective or ineffective lesson." The event may have been student work, which became, for the professor, secondary evidence of one's own professional performance. One other participant responded, "examining and reexamining my instruction, the projects I ask students to do, and the problems I ask them to solve." The event may have been a set of reviewer comments on a manuscript submitted for publication. A participant commented on an event, "reviewer comments on articles and paper proposals, reading research and attending conferences." Neverthe-less, for these professors, there was clearly a precipitating experience linked to a subsequent cognitive processing. This observation supports Schön's (1987) localization of the reflective act in practice itself, and not in technical rationality or knowledge-about.

This observation, that reflection must follow a practice event, suggests that one doesn't learn *how or about* practice, but *through and in* practice, a finding well-grounded in research on other professional groups but not on college faculty until this study. This fact immediately focuses a harsh light on professional development activities, which are divorced from active engagement with practice events for college faculty.

Typical activities for development for these professionals were confer-ence attendance and study leaves or sabbaticals, which are generally focused on academic specializations or content and not problems of prac-tice in higher education. A caveat here is that conferences can serve as the experiential basis for reflection, and so this generalization should be care-fully studied.

Discussion of Cognition Terminology

The actual event or incident triggered our participants to methodically think about the event that took place. One participant described the cog-nition this way, "it is those times that I am 'most in my own head.'" Our findings in this area illustrate the work of cognitive theorists such as Piaget, Vygotsky, and King and Kitchner.

Piaget argued that schemata are the cognitive or mental structures by which individuals intellectually adapt to and organize the environment (1954, as cited in Wadsworth, 2004). The individual can do one of two things: create a new schema in which to place the stimulus or modify an existing schema so that the stimulus fits into it. Both are forms of accom-modation and result in change in the configuration of one or more sche-mata. When disequilibrium occurs, it motivates the individual to seek equilibrium. This disequilibrium was described in affective terminology by respondents as expressions of lack of satisfaction with performance. Our participants focused on an event through contemplation, deconstruc-tion, or evaluative thinking. The combination of these steps in the event path created a sense of disequilibrium, which motivated them to then col-lect data through the use of tools (another component of the event path discussed later in this paper) to move toward a more balanced state. One of the participants described the cognitive process this way, "looking back at an event in an effort to ascertain why what went well, went well, and why what didn't go well, didn't. The goal is to build on the things that worked and rethink the aspects that didn't." Another participant stated, "Reflection is the process of self-examination and self-evaluation." "I define reflection as focused thinking about my teaching. I do this informally after each class by asking myself what went well."

Vygotsky (1996) believed that both thought and language were influenced by our sociocultural experience. The entire process was active and situated in the interaction and human connections of the sociocultural context (Wink & Putney, 2002). As described by the respondents, much of their reflection occurred, at some point, in a social context. Approximately 50% of the faculty felt the necessity to process the event with a confidant, someone they felt could guide or scaffold them through the cognitive process. One participant stated it this way, "I openly talk with colleagues about teaching situations that I do not feel were as successful as they should have been."

The narrative used by respondents was comprised of different developmental levels as described by King and Kitchner (1994). For example, a hunch is far more subjective than an analysis. One respondent stated, "Reflection is the process of contemplating the meaning, both personal and professional that can be found in a variety of data, artifacts, conversations and hunches." The different terms used by our respondents suggest they demonstrate different epistemic levels under the King and Kitchner model.

Discussion of Tools Terminology

The respondents selected ways to collect data to define their problem(s). We labeled this data collection as tools. Numerous studies confirm that tools are used as a form of data collection, aiding in bringing the event to reflection. Tools mentioned in the literature include: journaling, which involves writing down specific experiences, opportunities, and issues from practice; and/or introspection, trying to make sense of situations (Maloney & Campbell-Evans, 2002; Milner, 2003; Tillman, 2003). Additionally, tools include portfolios to help professionals analyze their teaching practices more consciously (Ellsworth, 2002; Marcoux, Brown, Irby, & Lara-Alecio, 2003; Willis, 2002). Approximately a third of our participants mentioned the use of journaling or some other tool that was private in nature. One participant commented, "I tend to do a lot of reflecting while I am commuting, but would like to begin journaling." Other participants stated, "a technique that I have found to be quite helpful is to try to do a written daily recap of each class that I teach" and "I keep a folder labeled 'next time' for each of the courses I teach."

Finally, critical dialogue tools, such as peer discussions or peer observations of teaching are social in nature: the reflection is being shared with others. Some respondents found it effective to use this form of data processing because it was a way to gain insight and/or feedback beyond oneself (Bell, 2001; DeBruin-Parecki & Henning, 2002; Hoban, 2000). The narratives provide examples of this type of tool. "I learn a great deal from student evaluations as well as direct comments from the students. Peer feedback provides another avenue for reflection." Another respondent stated, "Tools I use include peer evaluations of teaching and feedback from annual reviews" and "I consider the input of students and colleagues very serious. I actually set a time aside to do this when I am in a receptive mode."

Discussion of Change Point Terminology

No issue in professional practice has assumed greater importance over the last decade than the effectiveness of professional development. Nevertheless, the research is clear that much of this content gained through professional development has little impact on practice in most fields, and particularly teacher education. For our respondents, we observe a strong orientation toward change in future practice, particularly as this relates to their classroom teaching. Interestingly, this future change orientation is observed not only in junior rank faculty, for whom strong teaching evaluations are very important in this institution's faculty evaluation and promotion process, but also among tenured senior faculty members. Evidence of a possible change point was found in 14 of the 17 narratives. "Reflection is thinking about my teaching practice and analyzing what works well and where I need to make improvements. This has a major impact on my professional development." Yet another respondent made reference to "what I might change in the future." Several narratives referred to reflection as "thinking in an evaluative way about one's practice and making a plan to improve."

Our observation of change points immediately following cognitive activity, with subsequent trials of innovative practice solutions, suggests a single phenomenological pathway among our respondents. Our respondents, based on their reflective engagement with the prior event, develop an enhanced control over future experiences. This enhanced control is demonstrated by the change points found in their narratives and suggests affective growth in areas of confidence and satisfaction with self-development and professionalism. This was evidenced by one participant; he or she can "assess performance with an eye to improving both the student's experience and outcome. I do this using a tool I call self growth analyses."

According to Freire (1993) "Praxis is a complex activity by which individuals create culture and society, and become critically conscious human beings. Praxis comprises a cycle of action-reflection-action which is central to liberatory education" (pp. 83-85). The idea of praxis is directly related to our observation that change points are embedded in authentic reflection by college faculty in our participant group. Becoming critically conscious or self-aware is an idea that Schön, Dewey, and King and Kitchner have discussed as an important stage in professional development and maturation. Thus, the link between self-awareness through experience, reflection with successively more complex use of external input, and leading to change, is both credible from the research literature, and consistent with our data.

IMPLICATIONS

How do these findings impact the professional development of faculty with higher education? Briefly, if professors cannot or do not use tools to collect accurate and pertinent data, they will be limited in their success with reflection-based improvements of practice. In addition, determining the point of disequilibrium for an individual will be important to the successful sequencing of professional development during the career when professional development is based on personal reflection. Without some affective state of disequilibrium, there would tend not to be a motivation to begin the cognitive pathway. Finally, praxis can be viewed as the resolution of the disequilibrium resulting from the event trigger. In our case, the praxis can be viewed as either cognitive-leading to resolution of disequilibrium through behavior change, or praxis can be viewed as affective, with disequilibrium resolved into satisfaction following reflection and confirmation of success through the event. Refer to the other chapters for detailed explanation as to how each component of the reflective process is of value to the overall professional development of faculty in higher education.

QUESTIONS FOR INDIVIDUAL FOLLOW-UP

1. Define reflection.
2. How might this practice of reflection relate to your professional development as a faculty member?
3. Describe the tools you use to facilitate your reflection.

QUESTIONS FOR GROUP OR ORGANIZATIONAL CONSIDERATION

1. Does your organization include reflection as part of its core values and outcomes? If not, why? If so, how does the organization actually define reflection?

2. Does the organization outline a reflective process for faculty to follow?

CHAPTER 5

THE EVENT COMPONENT AS A PHENOMENOLOGICAL TRIGGER IN THE REFLECTION PATHWAY

Now a young professor in an education college, Brad nevertheless continued to structure his classes and his interpersonal relationships with students around a pivotal moment from earlier in his career when he briefly worked as a public school teacher. He had found a position in an urban elementary school working as a resource teacher to provide reading support to low socioeconomic level and highly at-risk students. Working as an intern, his supervising teacher at the school was a 40-year veteran. She had seen it all, it seemed. And whereas his university professors had emphasized methods and instructional strategies, this supervising teacher had but one word for Brad: relationship. For her, success in the classroom would be highly dependent upon earning the respect of his students and their parents: communicating quickly and consistently to these students and parents that he was "on their side," that he was respectful of their life struggles, that he was making every effort to help them succeed. And for his supervising teacher, the first step in this process was learning each students' name and, to the very best of his ability, something about them personally.

Years later in his role as a "doctored" professor, Brad had nevertheless embedded this truism deep into the fabric of his professional practice. Each semester, in every section, his first course of action was meeting his students, learning their names, and learning what motivated them personally as students and as young adults.

Reflection and the College Teacher: A Solution for Higher Education
pp. 57–70

And it paid off: Brad regularly received highly positive evaluations from his students that described, not only the rigor of his academic expectations, but the personally respectful and supportive tone that he created in his classes.

REVISING REFLECTION IN PRACTICE

One could argue that all professional educators, as with all adults, *think*. However, not all teachers are equally adept at posing, analyzing, and solving problems; nor do all teachers recognize good teaching practices such that the practice can be sustainably replicated. That being said, a highly developed disposition for analytical and reflective thinking promotes teacher development and contributes to enhanced student learning (Danielson, 2008).

In teacher education, reflective practice supports teachers as they move from routine actions in their teaching to more considered, cognitive actions. This transformation through reflection makes teachers "better" or at the very least aware of their pedagogical beliefs and practices (Vallance, 2006). Choulier, Picard, and Weite (2007, p.15) described reflection as the attitude adopted by an individual in order to take an external and critical look at his or her activity (in progress or completed). It allows teachers to analyze the contextual and generic elements of a situation, to gain a critical distance in relationship to the schemas being used, and to capitalize on past successes and failures to create a more successful future.

According to Lyons, (2006) reflection is an intentional act of mind, engaging a person alone or in collaboration with others in interrogating one's teaching, especially a compelling or puzzling situation of teaching or learning to construct some understanding of it. Others have discussed reflective practice as an iterative process that seeks to compare teaching practice to theories of action, and to adjust practice accordingly. Thus, reflection on teaching goes beyond mere evaluation in that it involves the process, ideas, assumptions and beliefs behind the action and fails to examine students' opportunities to learn merely from the perspective of products and outcomes (Bernacchio, Ross, Washburn, Whitney, & Wood, 2007; Hammersley-Fletcher & Orsmond, 2005; Kuit, Reay, & Freeman, 2001, p. 57). Other researchers do not assume that improving *how one teaches* always necessitates reflection. They assume, however, that reflection on one's teaching is likely to raise the question of how one teaches and in the end; this activity will have a positive effect on the improvement of teaching (Hubball, Collins, & Pratt, 2005, p. 60).

Reflection begins with one's perplexity about a topic and the willingness to adopt an attitude of suspended conclusion while studying the issue, gathering information, and gaining new knowledge. This reflection affords teachers conscious, deliberate insight to bring about enhanced student learning, and encourages teachers to become students of their own professional actions (Danielson, 2008, p. 130).

THE EVENT AS THE INITIAL PHENOMENA IN THE REFLECTION PATHWAY

Previously, we introduced the Wlodarsky-Walters Event Pathway. The research underlying this model confirms that for college faculty, reflection is a multidimensional process. The reflective path that we observed was driven by an *event* that was primarily a classroom teaching experience for our participants, and was fundamentally evaluative in nature. All of our respondents described the event using language that connoted evaluation, judgment, assessment of quality, success or failure.

THE EVENT

The importance of an authentic, phenomenological *event* as the motivational stimulus for reflection leading to change in professional practice cannot be overstated. This is the conceptual bedrock that allows a discussion of learning in or through practice, as opposed to learning about practice in a depersonalized manner or merely studying the professional as a developmental or existential adult out of the context of professional life. This type of thought was termed technical rationality by Schön (1983, 1987), whose works are the basis for much of contemporary thought on reflection. For Schön, the professional must expand upon technical understandings of the field of practice by an elaboration of experience through reflection-on, reflection-in and reflection-for authentic practice experiences. Reflection-on-action occurs after the action has been completed and is a look back on experience to better understand it. Reflection-in-action occurs during unique situations requiring problem solving in the midst of the experience. Reflection-for-action occurs when the individual begins to anticipate situations before being faced with them and/or begins to plan for the future to improve the present situation or outcome. Schön's contributions have fundamentally altered the structure of professional schools. In education one observes the incorporation of reflection as a major standard area under accreditation requirements for example, and explains as much as any theoretical foundation beyond Dewey's (1933) importance of problem-based professional development.

THE EVENT IN LITERARY TERMS

Campoy (2000) expanded the idea of the event using the term *opportunity* (p. 34). The *opportunity* is an integral step in reflection. As such, professional development must be linked to authentic experiences. This allows individuals to move from lower level, descriptive or scientific/definitional "retellings" toward more truly reflective, future-oriented understandings of practice.

This notion of the *event*, or Campoy's *opportunity*, is sustained and greatly expanded by King and Kitchner (1994) in their earliest (Stages 1 and 2) levels of reflective practice. For professionals at these levels, there is "an assumption that knowledge is gained through direct personal *observations*," that is, direct personal experience. This language is consistent with Campoy and Schön, and is also consistent with our identification of the practice event. Thus, our label *event* is conceptually identical to Campoy's *opportunity*, King and Kitchner's *observation* and Schön's *professional action*. The similarity of the underlying phenomenon for each of these terms across each of these lines of research enhances the credibility of these earlier studies as well as our current research and, now, focuses on the event itself.

THE EVENT IN PRACTICE

For our participants, their process of professional development as college faculty members began with an incident, an event of practice. This event may have been a class session or a set of classes over a semester period; it may have been a set of reviewer comments on a manuscript submitted for publication or it may have been student work which became, for the professor, secondary evidence of her own professional performance. Nevertheless, for these professors, there was clearly a precipitating experience linked to a subsequent cognitive processing. This observation supports Schön's localization of the reflective act in practice itself, and not in technical rationality or knowledge-about.

This observation, that reflection must follow a practice event, suggests that one does not learn *how or about* practice, but *through and in* practice, a finding well-grounded in research on other professional groups but not on college faculty until this study. This fact immediately focuses a harsh light on professional development activities which are divorced from active engagement with practice events for college faculty.

Typical events for development for these professionals are conference attendance and study leaves or sabbaticals, which are generally focused on academic specializations or content and not problems of practice in higher education. Other events, such as reading books and research, participation in discussion groups and learning communities, or attendance at lecture events are valuable for cognitive development. Nevertheless, they may be insufficiently linked to pedagogical and androgogical performance, the ability to write and perform research, or the skills and knowledge necessary for service as a faculty member. A caveat here is that conferences or other similar events can serve as the experiential basis for reflection, and so this generalization should be carefully studied.

AN ONTOLOGY OF EVENT

Because of the criticality of the event, as noted in this literature, as the precipitating or initiating first step toward reflection, we perceive a gap in current literature for a sustained focus and discussion of the nature and characteristics of the event, and a discussion of the implications of a critical event for professional development. Thus, we developed this chapter as a refinement of our initial model presented in earlier chapters with this more nuanced and careful description of that first step in the event path.

We perceive two distinct categories of events; one is termed *authentic,* and the other *reproduced,* following Benjamin's discussion of authenticity and reproduction of phenomena in his classic 1934 essay, *Art in the Age of Mechanical Reproduction.* Benjamin described the *aura* of an authentic object or phenomena as derived from its proximity in time and space to individual lives. We borrow this terminology and discussion as it pertains to our evolving understanding of professional reflection (Wlodarsky, 2005, 2009, 2010; Wlodarsky & Walters, 2006, 2007). In our *Event Path for Professional Reflection,* the process begins with an event. We accept that not all *authentic* events result in reflection, nor do we argue that a *reproduced* event necessarily will not. Our discussion will eventually unfold the issue of *authentic* or *reproduced* events and whether this distinction may affect differences in outcomes of the reflection path. An aside in this discussion seems needed: the epistemological fog of extreme postmodernism has obscured the distinctions between objective realism and subjective experience. Some, such as Allard et al. (2007) incorrectly and unhelpfully insert such discussions as:

> Too often, this word [authenticity] is used to suggest that authentic means some type of truth that can be stably accessed. Authentic becomes a term to suggest the teller knows the one true meaning about personal experience. Studies of memory and narrative demonstrate that, as we tell and retell our stories, they change and transmute, suggesting truth is being regularly modified and created. This process puts into question the notion of a stable type of truth. (p. 309)

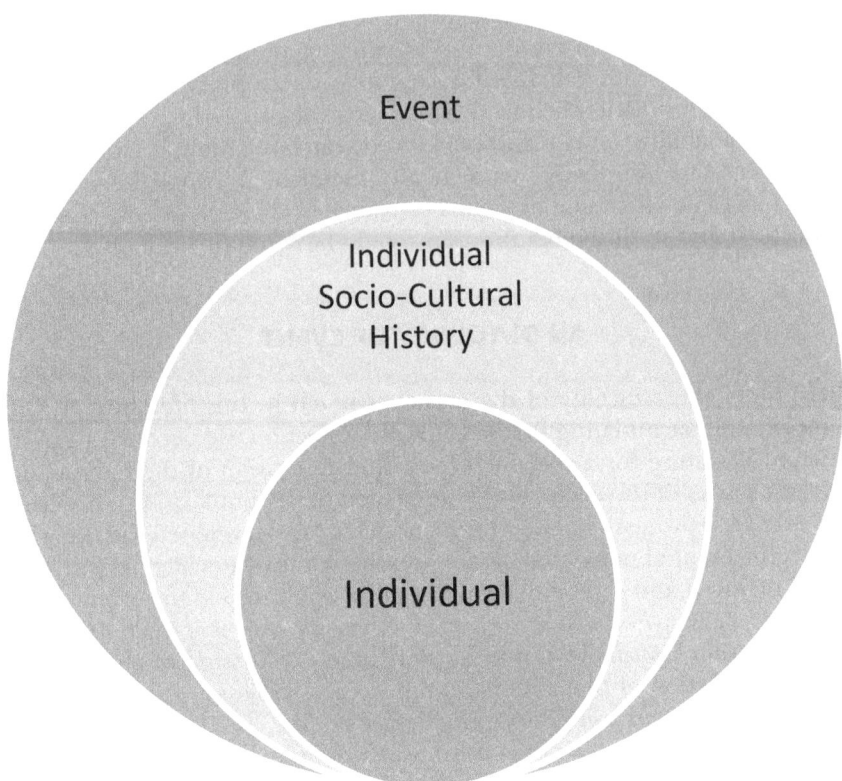

Figure 5.1.   The authentic event.

We avoid linking authenticity with objectivity/existential subjectivity in terms of truth claims and the interpretation of experience whether objective or subjective, in favor of linking authenticity to historicity (space and time). Thus, an event is construed as *authentic* when the individual is embedded in time and space with the event, which is thus directly apprehended through the senses, as in Figure 5.1. This is not to say that the individual's perception is not skewed by personal sociocultural history. In fact, it is to assert exactly that: the *authentic* event is a nexus of the event itself, the individual, and the historical and sociocultural life of the individual articulating in a singularity (Baudrillard, 1981/1994).

Figure 5.1 diagrams the *reproduced* event. This event is defined as *reproduced* when the individual and his or her sociocultural history is removed from a historical (time and space) relationship with the event itself such that it was not or cannot be experienced by that individual directly. Again,

Figure 5.2.   The reproduced event.

Benjamin might suggest that the event, in this instance, lacks the aura or patina of historical or biographical reference.

As we've worked through several of our own analyses and interpretations as well as a broad literary frame, we have developed our working definition of reflection:

> Reflection is a multifaceted construct comprised from different types of events—authentic or reproduced—which are experienced both through and outside of the individual and his or her sociocultural history. It is further understood that the cognitive process occurs on a continuum of subjective to objective based upon the tools incorporated in cognition.

Consequently, the distinction between the *authentic* and the *reproduced* event results in a dichotomy of more subjective (*authentic*) or more objective (*reproduced*) which is created from a singularity, or lack thereof, of the individual's sociocultural history in time and space with the event. Likewise, the cognitive process is dichotomized into more subjective (a lack of information derived from the use of data collection tools) or more objective (through information derived from the use of data collection tools). These dichotomies occur independently of each other due to the innate variability of experiences for the individual and the preparation for or knowledge of cognitive tools, suggesting that elements of the earlier *Event Path* (Wlodarsky & Walters, 2006) are more nuanced and complex as diagrammed in Figure 5.3. In this chart, the *authentic* event (because it includes the sociocultural history of the individual) is consequently more subjective. The *reproduced* event (because it does not include the sociocultural history of the individual) is consequently more objective. Cognition is then skewed more or less subjectively or objectively depending on the use of outside information collected systematically by the individual through the use of some cognitive tool (Wlodarsky, 2009, 2010). In Wlodarsky's (2009) analyses of cognitive tools used for reflection, it is clear that, with respect to these cognitive tools, the appropriateness of the tool and one's ability to use the tool will affect a subjective or objective stance for cognition.

THE SUBJECTIVE-OBJECTIVE DICHOTOMY OF THE EVENT

In this emerging reconceptualization of our event path (Figure 5.3), the newly revealed complexity of the process with respect to the nature of the event itself creates a series of questions and possibilities for outcomes deriving from the nature of the event and the eventual reflection. Whereas other researchers (King & Kitchener, 1994) have suggested that the individuals themselves are arrayed on a developmental continuum of more or less reflective, we suggest that differences in reflective thinking are derived, not only from some stage or phase of capability inherent in the individual adult, but also from differences in the nature of events and subsequent cognitive processing. The apparent differences in reflection can be explained by differences in the nature of the event and the emerging dichotomies of subjectivity and objectivity (which produce differentially weighted proofs in the mind of the individual if we view this epistemologically), and the eventual degree to which the individual can reembed the response to the event into his or her biography, following Schutz (1967) and Jarvis (2006a, 2006b). Based on our discussion, we have identified the multivarious complexities of event and outlined them in Figure 5.3. These complexities suggest a more nuanced view of the original event path. Each of these complexities may or may not lead even-

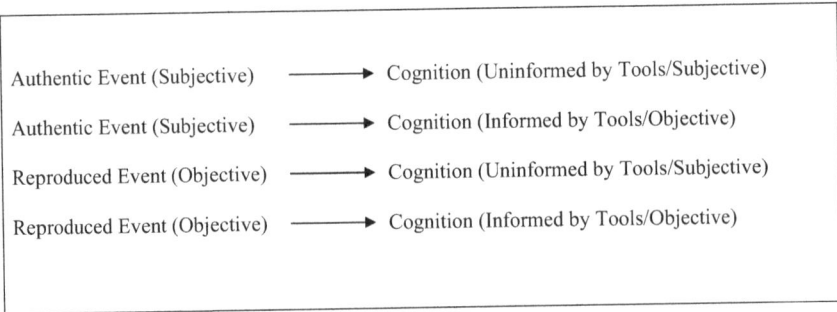

Figure 5.3.   The refined event.

tually to reflection. However, expressing these complexities as possibilities is a more realistic description of human experience.

IMPLICATIONS AND CAVEATS TO AN EVENT TYPOLOGY

As we have worked through this conceptualizing process for more accurately describing the event component in our reflective path, it has become clear to us that this identified complexity raises questions for further discussion. It is also clear to us that there are implications for professional practice and for situating and describing the broader event path that should be considered. These broader implications are several; however we choose to focus on three of them:

1. Whether the event is authentic or reproduced, it is more likely to result in reflection when it occurs to an individual with a predisposition toward reflectivity. This predisposition has been described as an innate value system or an existential way of being (Birmingham, 2003; Le Cornu, 2009) wherein reflection has been described as a moral characteristic of an individual.

We have invested much of this chapter in more carefully describing the event as the precipitating trigger for a path that the professional follows leading to reflection and a subsequent adoption of refined practice behaviors or a reconceptualization of self as a professional. In either case, the *authentic* or the *reproduced* event, the individual professional must be receptive to learning from experience. This receptivity has been characterized in two ways at least: attitude or preparation for a response, and disposition or developmental readiness for a response (C. Rogers, 2002).

Reflective practice can be described as the attitudes adopted by an individual in order to take an external and critical look at his/her activity, in progress or completed (Choulier et al., 2007). Wong, Yung, Cheng, Lan, and Hodson (2006) argued that if teachers are presented with problem-framed cases, they are naturally drawn into self-reflective inquiry. This concurs in Cochran-Smith's (2003) view of professional development as a process of helping teachers develop an attitude of inquiry toward their own teaching and learning. Evans (1985) claimed that reflectivity and lifelong learning are seen as remedies to uncertainty: "it leads to pedagogy which advocates that according the learner the responsibility to participate in shaping the purpose and process of learning is the most effective route to motivation and personal development" (p. 26).

The prevailing notion is "a commitment to oneself which calls for the acceptance of responsibility for one's own development" (Bagnall, 2006,

p. 260). Korthagen and Vasalos (2005) argue for a multilevel learning approach, which invites teachers to think about specific events in their teaching and to engage in a process called core reflection. The idea behind core reflection is that a teacher's core personality, including his or her identity and mission, profoundly influences the way that teacher practices.

In this light, the nature of the event may ultimately lead to reflection, but the nature of the individual can both enable and constrain the power of the event whether that event is *authentic* or *reproduced*.

2.   An event is often authenticated by organizational climate, policy and politics (Wlodarsky & Walters, 2006). Often this authentication centers on the evaluative structures in an organization. In this way, the reproduced event has the potential to function with respect to creating reflectivity as if it were authentic.

Contrived field experiences such as those in licensure programs in colleges are perhaps inadequate to serve as *authentic*, phenomenological events for reflection where the term is used as we have above because the historicity (genuineness in space and time) of these experiences is at least suspect. Nevertheless, it is possible that highly structured grading and evaluation procedures that potentially result in punitive or negative consequences could invest these field experiences with sufficient cognitive and emotional weight to force meaningful reflection. In this view, although the event may lack historicity and thus be questioned as *authentic*, the aura or patina of history can find its substitute in the historicity of the grades assigned to the response. This response may be pseudo-reflective in this case in the same way the event is pseudo-historical, but the outcome may be the same.

The learning society and the need for "learning systems" are concepts used to make sense of a process of change. Such concepts connote growth and development which are intrinsically good, but also misleading, according to Jarvis (2006a, 2006b), as they relate to changes driven by economic and market priorities (read evaluative or punitive) rather than naturalistic processes of human learning.

Reflective practice is not spontaneous (Stump & Donnel, 2002) but rather implies a conscious act (Stemfple & Badke-Schaub, 2002). Annetts and Kell (2009) found an underlying communication and induction problem between existing and newly recruited members of staff. They stated "While the department prided itself on an established commitment to and engagement with 'professional reflection,' it was guilty of policy holding and complacency" (p. 68). This study demonstrated the problems associated with assumed cultural practice and socialization where organizational climate interferes, potentially, with reflection and can ascribe greater cultural importance to experiences that are not essentially *authentic*.

Lyons (2006) found that several factors interact in the activities of the teachers within her study. First, their own personal histories of teaching and learning influence their starting place, what they believe teaching to be. Then, the university itself provides a significant, new institutional context for validating discussions of teaching and learning. Last, ongoing seminars provide a scaffold for inquiry into one's teaching, a critical support for bringing to consciousness new insights into ones teaching and student learning (p.165).

Hubball et al. (2005) suggested that faculty developers should pay particular attention to the bigger picture of institutional norms in which faculty are situated, work toward developing an academic culture that values reflective teaching practices, ensure that there is adequate time for reflection within the context of a faculty development program and, finally, through individualized prior learning assessment, develop clear expectations and goals for reflection experiences that ideally build toward a summative document or an appropriate assignment that helps integrate reflective activities (p. 78). Andreu et al. (2003) argued that one of the most important features is the creation of a nonevaluative environment where participants feel safe to raise questions about their own and others' work.

In a study completed by Vallance (2008), among the many findings, two are relevant to our discussion of the sociocultural impact on the event. Vallance found that all students had input a lot of text outside class time, possibly due to the allocation of a course grade component, a sociocultural impact on the event. In addition, when asked if the students would use the software again in the future as a way to reflect, results indicated that the majority would not. A possible explanation could be that the students only used the software because they were required to in order to earn a reasonable grade for the course. Finally, Hobbs (2007) found from her own experience and research that even where a supportive environment rather than the grade is prioritized, individuals, by nature, tend to believe that writing ideas that their superiors agree with or view as intelligent and meaningful will have a positive effect on their grade or position.

With respect to the nature or type of event, whether *authentic* or *reproduced*, it is clear from the findings across this selection of research that the event itself and the very path toward reflection is highly influenced by the sociocultural and political expectations of the practice environment. This skew will only enhance again the complexity of the pathway from any type of event toward closure and professional reengagement in practice.

3. The eventual degree to which the individual can reembed the response to the event into his or her biography is contingent upon the degree to which the event is authentic/subjective or reproduced/objective, following Schutz (1967) and Jarvis (2006a, 2006b).

As individuals, we do bring biases to our interpretation of experiences. Nevertheless, interpretation is not the extent of our reality. By nature, some events are historical for us and carry the epistemological weight of our direct sensory input. Some events are not historical, rather they are retellings and scenarios and the stories of others recast for our use and potential learning. It seems to us that the historic distance of the precipitating event from our lives may be a direct measure, though an abstract one, of the distance we must cover to reembed the lessons learned through the experience into our responses in future, similar events. This notion is quite abstract but closes for us this chapter as an intellectual exercise.

Authentic events are already embedded in our personal histories and biographies by definition. We have directly lived these events. *Reproduced* events, regardless of relevance to professional practice, are encountered secondarily at best with respect to our personal history and biography. Although these *reproduced* events may serve as powerful and useful triggers for the subsequent event path and may lead to deep growth and reconceptualizations of both self and practice, they will necessitate greater work. Their effect, if we may grasp a statistical metaphor, is diffused over greater historical distance and must therefore be more powerful to produce the same effect as a direct, historically perceived, *authentic* event.

CONCLUSION

In this chapter we have brought focus, through discussion and a selective incorporation of relevant literature and our research as background, to the event that triggers a process leading to professional reflection. In this discussion, we have identified a theoretical and philosophical basis for categorizing these events dichotomously, the conceptions of reality and experience developed by Benjamin in his work in the 1930s and later, and the work of Baudrillard around authenticity and simulation. Such a discussion reveals that our earlier work on the process of reflection inadvertently masked a greater complexity for understanding the elements in this path, as well as the overall model itself. As our body of research has developed and evolved, we have identified a more accurate depiction of the real connections between lived experience, cognition (Chapter 6), and change (Chapter 8) that are embedded in professional reflection, but do reveal that much of what we know about adult learning and change in institutions such as colleges of education is simplistic and immature. Certainly the more complex view of the precipitating event suggests that later considerations such as the disposition of the individual, the sociocultural and political environment, and the personal life of the individual, are ever more complex and more deeply connected to the outcomes than our model and the models of others suggest.

QUESTIONS FOR INDIVIDUAL FOLLOW-UP

1. Individuals are always shaped emotionally, professionally, and personally by significant life events that leave a mark on them. Find a quiet place, and some time to invest in thinking (maybe a coffee shop), and on a clean piece of notebook paper, review your life. What key events transformed you? Were there tragedies? Triumphs? Accomplishments? Key interactions with others? Note these for later thought.

2. With the list you developed in the initial question above, how might these life events contribute to the professional choices you are making now? How might you harness the power of these experiences to your own professional development? Are there problems in practice you seem to consistently struggle with? Can you link these two key events in your past where this pattern of behavior may have been created?

3. How do you know when an event may ultimately prove critical in your developing conception of personal and professional self-awareness? How do you record or document your daily, weekly, monthly, and/or yearly experiences so as to provide self-monitoring of the events that may ultimately shape your thinking?

QUESTIONS FOR GROUP OR ORGANIZATIONAL CONSIDERATION

1. What critical events occur on the various timetables of your organization (perhaps deadlines, recurring reports, etc.) and how are these incorporated into data collection and analysis for your assessments?

2. The various assessment reports that are created in most organizations are important "touchpoints" for documenting events. How are these disseminated throughout the constituency of your organi-

zation so that everyone, from the grassroots and up, has the benefit of this type of documentation?

3. What events are documented as a required part of employee evaluations? Are there standardized forms for these? Are there other key events that can be anticipated with regularity which are currently absent from this documentation?

CHAPTER 6

COGNITIVE PROCESSING OF INFORMATION

In 2005, as research partners we decided to copresent a paper on the reflective practitioner in higher education at an adult learning conference. We had been working on our line of research for a couple of years and were excited to present some findings from our research on reflective practice to our colleagues. We had invested significant time reviewing the literature on reflection only to find that, although this topic was certainly being investigated, there were still substantive questions to be answered. We were excited to share the relationship between the characteristics of reflection on practice and pertinent, personal and career-related demographics of faculty members. Although we had some initial results, we acknowledged that there was still much to learn about reflection. For this reason, we decided to participate in the roundtable format at the conference to facilitate a discussion on the topic of reflection for the purposes of providing us with feedback on our work. We did not realize at the time the interaction that took place during the roundtable would have a profound effect on our research agenda. One of the attendees of our roundtable happened to be a faculty member who sat on one of our dissertation committees. As he listened attentively to our presentation, we were feeling confident in our work when he "popped" a question that really forced us to step back and take a closer look at our research on reflection. The question he posed to us was, "what is this thing called reflection? Isn't it just thinking about something? How is reflection different from thinking?" As simple as the question was, it was profound. It compelled us to take a step back and really make sure we had a strong understanding of the definition of reflection, and how (and if) it is different from "just thinking" before we continued to research anything else about reflection. Our

Reflection and the College Teacher: A Solution for Higher Education
pp. 71–82
Copyright © 2014 by Information Age Publishing

71

research eventually lead to our writing a definition of reflection, and an operational model for reflection (Chapter 4) which includes the cognition component. Once cognition was identified as part of the reflective process or event path and researched thoroughly (Wlodarsky & Walters, 2007), the question was answered for us, "thinking" is NOT the same as reflection.

THINKING ≠ REFLECTION

To clarify, thinking is just one component of reflection, or the reflective process. The process of reflection includes additional components that make it distinct from thinking. Rather, we argue that thinking, the term used by our colleague in the story above, resembles a different term; cognition: which is only one of several components within the reflective process, or event path. In other words, thinking and reflection are not conceptual synonyms.

As mentioned in the previous chapters, the event path begins with a precipitating *Event*, followed by an intentional period of *Cognitive* processing of information. The *Cognition* component serves as the point in which the problem is formulated. The actual event or incident triggered our participants to methodically think about the event that took place. This chapter focuses on the component of cognition, or thinking as part of the event path (Wlodarsky & Walters 2007).

Loughran's (1996) notion of reflection confirms that reflection and thinking are different. Loughran believes that reflection is a purposeful, deliberate act of inquiry into one's thoughts and future actions through which a perceived problem is examined in order that a thoughtful, reasoned response might be tested out (p. 221). Moon (1999, p. 62) further suggested that reflection implies a form of mental processing with a purpose and/or anticipated outcome that is applied to relatively complicated or unstructured ideas for which there is not an obvious solution. Gelter (2003) defined reflection as a conscious, active process of focused and structured thinking which is distinct from free floating thoughts, as in general thinking or day dreaming. In this view, reflection could not be the same as thinking because the definition includes the notion of *future action*. Although thinking or cognition is only one component of the process, it is an integral part of the process, and needs to be examined closely for understanding.

COGNITION WITHIN THE REFLECTIVE PROCESS

Boyd and Fales (1983, p. 100) defined reflective learning as "the process of *internally examining* and exploring an issue of concern, triggered by an experience, which creates and clarifies meaning in terms of self and which results in a changed conceptual perspective." Boud, Keogh, and Walker (1985, p. 5) viewed reflection as "a generic term for those *intellectual and affective activities* in which individuals engage to explore their experiences in order to lead to new understandings and appreciation." Both of these definitions include terms that imply that there is a cognitive process taking place—internally examine and intellectual activity.

According to Mezirow (2000), after a disorienting dilemma that sets the process in motion, the learner engages in *self-examination* that is often accompanied by feelings of fear, anger, guilt or shame (p. 22). Brookfield (2000) argued that critical reflection is central to transformative learning—an act of learning can be called transformative only if it involves a fundamental *questioning and reordering of how one thinks* or acts (p. 139).

Gelter (2003) implied that there may be a genetic predisposition for reflection in the brain that facilitates the generating of relevant thoughts for reflection. As the growth of neurons is largely epigenetic (having an external origin, not genetic) it is more plausible that reflection is a learned process of an unconscious selecting of spontaneously generated thoughts that are metaphorically "bent" back into the conscious focus while nonrelevant thoughts are left to fade away.

Kolb (1984) talked about two modes of grasping the world. These correspond to the two dimensions in the learning process as the concrete experiencing of events and the *abstract conceptualization* of it. The first is called apprehension and is a way of summarizing our sensations, whereas the second is called comprehension and is a way of introducing order in such sensations and making them communicable. This model corresponds well with our event path; we describe an event as well; an apprehension followed by an abstract conceptualization or, as we refer to it, cognition, the process of knowing or comprehending.

WHAT IS COGNITION AND ITS CONNECTION TO LEARNING?

The literature almost makes it impossible to discuss cognition separate from learning. For this reason, our discussion about cognition, throughout this chapter, includes the notion of learning. We are not arguing that cognition is learning, rather that cognition is part of the learning process.

The literature tends to be organized around philosophies of learning, one of which is cognitivism. Cognitive theories focus not on behavioral outcomes but on the *thought* processes involved in human learning. In other words, cognitive theories focus on "how we think" rather than on how we learn. As Winch said, "cognitivism is not only a set of theories about how people learn; it is also about how they think" (1998, p. 46, as cited in Ormrod, 2004, p. 163). Cognition is a major part of the learning process and for that reason, Winch elaborated on his definition of cognitivism:

> A solitary and a social theory of learning *par excellence*. Modern cognitivism holds that individual brains, acting as solitary units from birth, possessed of representational structures and transformation rules, and receiving "input" from the exterior, can account for the way in which we learn. (p. 157)

The cognitive perspective recognizes thinking, not exclusively behavior, as essential to understanding human nature, accomplishment and potential (Martinez, 2010). Martinez (2010) identified two broad classes of educational outcome-knowledge and the ability to think well—which capture much of what we hope for from educational experiences. They also constitute what an educated mind brings to a complex world. Martinez expresses these two broad mental capabilities in the words *learning* and *cognition*. We should promote the acquisition of knowledge (learning) but it should also nurture an ever increasing ability to think clearly, creatively, and productively (cognition) (2010).

Cognitivists would restrict their definition of learning to the process whereby the internal representations more clearly reflect the reality of the external world that they depict (Jarvis, 2006a, 2006b). Jarvis took a different view and did not restrict the use of the term "cognitive" to the way that the cognitivists use it, but rather is employing it to refer to the whole domain where thought plays a significant but not exclusive, role in the process of learning. We agree with Jarvis' argument that cognitive theory as an approach to learning is incomplete (Jarvis, 2006b, p. 162). Moreover, this omission removes a major reason for learning, to understand the world and when there is disharmony between what Jarvis calls biography and the life-world to reestablish that harmony.

Learning, according to Warhurst (2008), constitutes the development of various types of knowledge and modes of knowing and of new ways of acting, that is, of new ways of being in the world. Warhurst also defines reflection as involving a stepping back from experience, reviewing that experience through questioning and making sense of the experience through the construction of personal knowledge for practice.

Cognition or thinking is internal, so the question becomes, what is actually happening as someone thinks, as cognition is taking place. The literature on the psychoneurological pathways for cognition sheds some light on the activity of knowledge collection and processing.

COGNITION AND KNOWLEDGE COLLECTION/FORMATION

Epistemology, the theory of knowledge and knowing, is a branch of philosophy concerned with the nature of knowledge, its possibility, scope, general bias, and justification of belief (Honderich, 1995). For centuries, philosophers have grappled with three general areas of inquiry: the limits of human knowledge, the sources of human knowledge and the nature of human knowledge (Arner, 1972). Inquiry into the sources of human knowledge includes what the genuine sources of knowledge are, how knowledge is acquired and how knowledge is represented (Honderich, 1995).

We view the cognition component as a micro process that functions within the macro process of reflection. Cognition is a process whereby raw data is transformed into useful knowledge. We argue that useful knowledge about the event will lead to change or satisfaction with the event. Our experience as well as the literature indicates that individuals or organizations gather knowledge (data) from (a) an actual event, (b) content knowledge, or (c) other experiences. King (2002) defined reflection as a deliberate process when the candidate takes time within the course of their work to focus on their performance and think carefully about the thinking that lead to particular actions, what happened and what they are learning from *experience*, in order to inform what they might do in the future. Other researchers looked more closely at content knowledge. Another form of reflection which seems to lead to deeper learning involves adopting a critical stance including consideration of broader contexts, examining theoretical positions, asking fundamental questions and preparing for change (Hatton & Smith, 1995; Van Manen, 1977). In addition, Moon (2004) confirmed the importance of meta-cognition and revisiting material already learnt. This supports higher level learning processes, mulling over plans and theories and reflecting on implications. Finally, referring back to the discussion on working memory, it should be noted that there are individual differences in working memory. Individuals differ, of course, in the capacity of their working memories to accomplish a given learning task. One of the main factors in enhancing this capacity is background knowledge. In other words, the more a person knows about something, the better able the person is to organize and absorb new information. According to some researchers, other experiences help individuals gather knowledge. For those who hold the constructivist approach to experiential learning, cognition is a key component through which individuals extract knowledge from their concrete experiences (Fenwick, 2001; Illeris, 2007). They considered that individuals also differ in their abilities to organize information and therefore emphasize the importance of other experiences to knowledge collection.

To clarify this notion of cognition, we must gain a glimpse at the process that actually occurs as knowledge is being collected and/or formulated. This takes us to the literature on psychoneurological pathways for cognition.

PSYCHONEUROLOGICAL PATHWAY
FOR KNOWLEDGE COLLECTION/FORMATION

According to Slavin (2011), the human mind is a meaning maker. From the first second you see, hear, taste, or feel something, you start the process of deciding what it is, how it relates to what you already know and whether it is important to keep in your mind or should be discarded. What is the process by which information is absorbed? This question has been addressed by cognitive learning theorists and has led to what is known as the information processing theory. Atkinson and Shiffrin (1968) described a model of information processing that begins with external stimulus, or information that enters the brain. Once the external stimulus enters the brain, the sensory register holds it briefly as the decision is made as whether or not to pay attention to the information. This initial processing allows for the information to enter the short-term or working memory. This is the part of the memory in which information is currently being thought about; in other words, the thoughts we are conscious of having at any given moment. The working memory is where the mind operates on information, organizes it for storage or discarding, and connects it to other information (p. 161). Information may enter the working memory from the sensory registers or from the long-term memory. This is an important distinction because it allows individuals to *think* about information, or process knowledge that is familiar data (long-term memory) and/or new data (sensory register).

Piaget introduced the term "scheme" to describe a cognitive framework that individuals use to organize their perceptions and experiences. Cognitive processing theorists similarly use the terms schema and schemata to describe networks of concepts that individuals have in their memories that enable them to understand and incorporate new information. These findings, as well as many others, of brain research reinforce the conclusion that the brain is not a filing cabinet for facts and skills but is engaged in a *process* of organizing information to make it efficiently accessible and usable (Slavin, 2011).

Cognition, by no means, should be characterized as effortless; however, there are arguments for a more advanced way of thinking. The literature outlining a more complex cognition reveals characteristics similar to that of the *cognitive* component of the event path (Wlodarsky & Walters, 2007).

COMPLEX COGNITION

According to Martinez (1998), complex cognition is different from straightforward, simple, linear thinking. It is often multifaceted, evaluative, and open-ended. Examples of complex cognition include, but are not limited to: problem solving, critical thinking, inferential reasoning, creative thinking and metacognition.

Problem solving is the pursuit of a goal when the path to that goal is uncertain (Martinez, 1998; Mayer & Whittrock, 2006). Many goals cannot be achieved by following a set of rules: they are open-ended and complex; they are problems. The word problem doesn't necessarily mean something negative; rather, a problem is simply a goal whose attainment is not straightforward. This notion of problem aligns well with the *event* component of the event path. The notion of cognition is mentioned and intertwined with Brookfield's (1987) work on critical thinking. He summarized that critical thinking involves calling into question the assumptions underlying our customary, habitual ways of thinking and acting differently on the basis of this critical questioning. Brookfield talked about thinking being a process, not an outcome. He stated,

> Being critical thinkers entails a continual questioning of assumptions. People can never be in a state of complete critical development. If we ever felt that we had reached a state of fully developed or realized critical awareness, we would be contradicting one of the central tenets of critical thinking, namely that we are skeptical of any claims to universal truth or total certainty. By its nature, critical thinking can never be finished in some final, static manner. (p. 6)

Brookfield also discussed the components of critical thinking. It is a process of identifying and challenging assumptions. Once these assumptions are identified, critical thinkers examine their accuracy and validity. Part of this process also includes challenging the importance of the context; critically thinking allows us to be aware that practices, structures and actions are never context-free. Central to critical thinking is the capacity to imagine and explore alternatives to existing ways of thinking and living. This kind of cognition, or thinking, according to Brookfield, leads to reflective skepticism—do not take things as read. In other words, simply because a practice or structure has existed for a long time, does not mean that it is the most appropriate for all time, or even for this moment. Just because an idea is accepted by everyone else, does not mean that we have to believe in its innate truth without first checking its correspondence with reality as we experience it (Brookfield, 1987).

Inferential reasoning is based on the word inference, which is the cognitive act of going beyond the information given to draw a new conclusion; using the data available to generate a conclusion. Creative thinking can be characterized by divergent production, concentration on a created product, seeing old ideas in new ways, and combining ideas.

Metacognition is known as "thinking about thinking." Whenever we think about our own thought process, we are engaged in metacognition.

Metacognition tends to be quite conscious and deliberate. This description goes beyond simple thinking (Martinez, 2010). As we briefly described complex cognition, it appears to be closely aligned with the cognition that takes place within the event path; thinking that is *not* simple, linear, but rather a complex microprocess.

OUR DESCRIPTIONS OF COGNITION

Analysis of our original survey data, described in Chapter 4, indicated that reflection for the participants is an internal, cognitive process using the brain as the primary tool. The participants engaged in a cognitive process whereby awareness surfaced and a sense of knowing emerged. In short, they had to "think about" their experiences for some period of time. Although they were willing to listen to input from their peers, a significant part of the cognitive process was private, a process which no one else knew the hidden thoughts of the faculty member. Select narrative quotations in the original data set which support this theme include (Wlodarsky & Walters, 2006):

- "I use my two hour commute to **critically examine** why something was successful in my class and what may have impacted successes and failures."
- "I define reflection as **focused thinking** about my teaching. I do this informally after each class by asking myself what went well."
- "For me, I reflect in a more informal sense most especially in my car, or late at night. It is those times that I am **most in my own head**."
- Other participants described the cognitive process this way (Wlodarsky & Walters, 2006):
- "**Looking back** at an event in an effort to ascertain why what went well; went well, and why what didn't go well, didn't. The goal is to build on the things that worked and **rethink** the aspects that didn't."
- "Reflection is the process of **self-examination** and **self-evaluation**."

Other terms our respondents used included "ponder, mull over, examine, reexamine, and think about" to describe part of the reflective process. This circle of thought is cognition (Wlodarsky & Walters, 2006, 2007).

THINKING STYLES

How one chooses *to think* may certainly play a role in how efficiently and effectively one works through the reflective process. Therefore, a brief but important outline of the different thinking styles is necessary within this chapter.

Intellectual styles, a general term for various labels with the root word "style" such as cognitive styles, learning styles, and thinking styles, refer to people's preferred ways of processing information (Zhang & Sternberg, 2006). Although these styles are conceptually different, they are similar in a fundamental way. That is, all of them are different from abilities. Ability refers to what one can do. Whereas a style refers to how one prefers to use the abilities one has (Sternberg & Zhang, 2001). The process of thinking includes the representation and processing of information in the mind (Sternberg, 1997). Thinking style has been described as one's preferred manner of using mental abilities to govern daily activities, including understanding and solving problems and challenges. At least partially socialized, thinking styles may vary depending on the conditions and demands of a given situation (Sternberg, 1988). Sternberg (1988) proposed the theory of mental self-government and argued that there are many ways to govern our society, manage our activities or use our abilities. People flexibly use their mind for mental self-government to form a variety of thinking styles. This theory contends that as there are many ways of governing society, there are also many ways to govern or manage the thinking process. Different individuals use different thinking styles to govern new information and to approach and manage a learning task, choosing those styles with which they are comfortable (Zhang & Sternberg, 2000). More recently, the focus has been on seven styles: *conservative* preference to work on tasks that allow one to adhere to existing rules and procedures in performing tasks, *liberal* preference to work on tasks that involve novelty and ambiguity, *local* preference to work on tasks that require working with concrete details, *global* preference to pay more attention to the overall picture of an issue and to abstract ideas, *judicial* preference to work on tasks that allow for one's evaluation, as well as to evaluate and judge the performance of other people, *executive* preference to work on tasks with clear instructions and structures—implementation of tasks with established guidelines; and *legislative* preference to work on tasks that require creative strategies, choosing one's own activities (Zhang, 2004).

Felder and Silverman (1988) referred to the way students receive and process new information as learning styles. Learning styles describe the way that learners perceive, interact with and respond cognitively to the learning input. Characteristics of each style include *sensing*—concrete thinker, practical and oriented toward facts and procedures; *intuitive*—abstract thinker, innovative and oriented toward theories and underlying meanings; *visual*—prefers visual representations of presented material, such as pictures, diagrams and flow charts; *verbal*—prefers written and spoken explanations; *active*—learns by trying things out and enjoys working in groups; *reflective*—learns by thinking things through and prefers working alone or with a single familiar partner; *sequential*—learns in small incremental steps and uses linear thinking process; and *global*—learns in large leaps, holistic thinking process.

Vance, Groves, Paik, and Kindler (2011) defined a model where linear thinking style has a preference for attending to external, tangible data and facts and processing this information through conscious logic and rational thinking to form knowledge, understanding or a decision for guiding subsequent action. Nonlinear thinking styles is defined as a preference for attending to internal feelings, impressions, and sensations and processing this information (both consciously and unconsciously) through intuition, creativity, or insight to form knowledge, understanding, or a decision for guiding subsequent action.

Rowe and Mason (1987) developed a decision-style inventory, which measures for decision style types: directive, behavioral, analytic and conceptual. The directive and behavioral styles which emphasizes decision making based upon rules and policies, is consistent with the nonlinear thinking dimension. The analytical and conceptual decision styles are described as more cognitively complex decision styles (capable of handling greater ambiguity) that utilize various information sources (including intuition and insight), consider many alternatives and tend to emphasize ethics and values.

Eigenberger, Critchley, and Sealander (2007) took their investigation in a different direction. In addition to acknowledging that different thinking styles exist and may have an impact on the cognitive process, Eigenberger et al. went as far as to say more people are inclined to approach problematic situations with a certain attitude or style. The two styles include one characterized as favoring intellective approaches that rely on expansive inferential processes, governed by deductive and inductive rules and the other characterized as favoring naturally reactive, or default approaches that restrict inferential processes and aim at expedient judgment. Most people are inclined to approach problematic situations with the latter attitude reflecting confidence in the prejudgments that have been formed by instruction, self-interest, and stereotypes.

LIMITATIONS OF COGNITION COMPONENT

It is necessary to mention, briefly, the limitations of the cognition component to the reflective path. These limitations influence the extent to which an individual and/or organization successfully completes the cognition component of the reflective process. The limitations noted here are not comprehensive and may be added to as further research is completed.

The *first* limitation on cognition is the stress and/or emotion that can be tied to the event or problem being experienced. According to Starcke (2011), there is growing evidence that stress affects cognitive and emotional processes such as memory, attention and fear conditioning as well as simple decision making. Gray (1999) confirmed this argument in a study where students reporting stress due to impending exams showed a bias to short term thinking in a decision making task based on emotional feedback processing. In addition, recent neuropsychological studies also indicate that stress induced in the laboratory is related to decision making that leads to disadvantageous results in the long run (Starcke, 2011). Starcke, Wolf, Markowitsch, and Brand (2008) also observed that stress led to more risky choices in decision making. This was due to, in part, emotional feedback processing.

A *second* limitation involves disabilities. There are certain disabilities that may cause individuals to struggle with knowledge collection and formation. By definition, a disability is a functional limitation a person has that interferes with the person's physical or cognitive abilities (Slavin, 2011). This field of inquiry extends well beyond our discussion here, and the reader is encouraged to refer to research on specific disabilities.

As indicated in the previous section on thinking styles, individuals have a predisposition toward a style of thinking. This being true, individuals who have predispositions for certain styles of thinking may be challenged as they try to complete such cognitive processes. We suggest the reader review additional literature on thinking styles for more information.

Thus far, when discussing the event or problem being experienced, the individual is, to some extent, formulating the problem. How an individual or organization defines the event or problem would likely influence to what extent there is a need to work through the cognitive component of the process. For example, if the individual or organization views the problem as minor, they may choose not to continue with the reflective process. This brings us to the notion of commitment. Another limitation would be a lack of commitment toward the event, or problem being experienced. The individual or organization, even if the event is considered minor, may choose to participate in the reflective process; however, the commitment may be deficient.

A *fifth* limitation to consider is when individuals lack a retrieval mechanism to collect knowledge from long-term memory. As stated previously, information may enter the working memory from sensory registers or from long-term memory. This is an important distinction because it allows individuals to think about information, or process knowledge that is familiar data (long-term memory) and/or new data (sensory register). The limitation occurs when the individual struggles to find a retrieval mechanism that is successful in accessing information from long-term memory.

Not being able to retrieve information from long-term memory is an example of missing, or uniformed data. Information may also be missing externally, in other words, not all the information from the problem itself has been identified. In addition to missing information, the individual or organization may be receiving bad or ill-informed data. In either case, this is a *sixth* limitation of the cognition component.

QUESTIONS FOR INDIVIDUAL, GROUP, OR ORGANIZATIONAL FOLLOW-UP AND/OR CONSIDERATION

1. Where is the knowledge you are collecting coming from? Describe in detail, that is, event, content, other experiences.
2. Once you have identified the problem (event), do you define it as minor or major? What is your commitment to solving the problem?
3. What is your thinking style? How might this impact your cognitive process?
4. Are there any stress and/or emotion connected to the problem? Describe in detail. How might you deal with this so that it does not hinder the cognitive process?
5. Are there any disabilities, things that may hinder the cognitive process that you need to take into consideration?
6. Are you familiar with retrieval mechanisms? If not, you may want to investigate some possible strategies for retrieving information as a way to help facilitate the cognitive process.
7. Can you think of any information that may be missing, inaccurate?

CHAPTER 7

TOOLS THAT HELP PROFESSIONALS FACILITATE THE REFLECTIVE PROCESS

As early as I can recall, when asked to "reflect" for a class assignment, I was to do so by way of journaling. Teachers often made reflection an assignment: make a journal, decorate the cover, and personalize it. Although I enjoyed this part of reflection, I hated the actual act of writing my thoughts down on paper. Sometimes the assignment called for me to answer specific questions, which caused me to wondered, "Is this true reflection if I have to answer specific questions?" At other times, I was able to freely write whatever I wanted. In this instance, I often struggled to get something, anything, on paper and I often felt uncomfortable having my teacher read my journal entries. During my many years of schooling, I did not enjoy journaling, and therefore never embraced the act of journaling. More importantly, I walked away from these journaling experiences believing that I didn't know how to reflect; that I wasn't "good" at it. And if I was <u>forced</u> to journal, I found myself going through the process simply as a means to an end. After finishing school, I avoided journaling all together!

Although I believed in the importance of reflection, I found myself not being very reflective because I hated journaling and didn't find it productive. At the same time, I had a desire to grow as a professional (and personally too), to challenge myself, to find ways to confirm that what I was doing was effective and to be accountable to what was ineffective. I just needed to figure out how to grow personally and professionally without having to journal. Does this mean that journaling isn't an effective tool to reflect? No. I have realized that the tool used to reflect can

Reflection and the College Teacher: A Solution for Higher Education
pp. 83–91

make the difference in whether or not the reflection is successful. I asked myself the question, "are there other tools to facilitate reflection and if so, what are they?" I soon found out that there are many other ways to reflect that are enjoyable to the individual as well as productive. As I look back on my journaling experiences, I now know that journaling can and is a very helpful tool in facilitating reflection. It simply wasn't the tool for me and/or my situation. I tend to be a very social person so journaling made me feel isolated. I prefer to share with others in hopes of creating a productive dialogue, which will ultimately lead to my developing as a professional.

—Mrs. Jane Doe
Sixth-Grade Science Teacher

IMPORTANCE

In a report published by the U.S. Department of Education (2006), concern exists that the quality of student learning at U.S. colleges and universities is inadequate and, in some cases, declining. It was found that the results of scholarly research on teaching and learning are rarely translated into practice, especially for those working in fields such as teacher preparation. The U.S. Department of Education recommends that colleges and universities embrace a culture of continuous innovation and quality improvement by developing new pedagogies, curricula, and technologies to improve learning.

Education professionals can begin to address this recommendation if they intentionally choose to reflect on their practice(s). To confirm the importance of reflection, the National Council for Accreditation of Teacher Education (2008) commented on the notion of reflection by stating (see Standard 5 of the Unit Assessments), that faculty should "reflect on their own practice."

Professional growth requires the understanding that individuals are different and their working conditions are unique. This must be taken into consideration as we study professional development. If we really want to help individuals grow, we will have to find ways that fit their wiring; growth is hand crafted, not mass produced. We argue that college faculty and other professionals must search out what reflective tools are available and suitable for them, tool(s) that are likely to be effective in facilitating their reflection.

With the need for more reflective individuals and organizations obvious, we believed it was important to dedicate a chapter of this book to describing some of the tools and characteristics associated with these tools that may be helpful to professionals who want to learn more about the reflective process.

INTRODUCTION

What purpose does the tool component serve in the event path? Are there tools that appear to be more useful to the individual and/ organization? How might the practice of using specific tools aid in the professional development of an individual and/or organization? We scrutinized the reflective tools through the experiences of faculty surveyed and then summarized the characteristics associated with certain tools (refer to Table 7.1). These tools include: (a) peer feedback in which the event is *not* directly observed, (b) peer feedback in which the event is directly observed, (c) journaling, (d) student input, and (e) shared research through conference presentations and publications.

Tool 1: Peer Feedback, Event Not Directly Observed

Faculty members mention relying on colleagues for feedback on events they experienced. Often, when a colleague provides feedback, he or she has not witnessed the event directly and therefore relies on the event being defined by the faculty member who experienced it. For example, a faculty member commented during a group discussion on student participation,

> Participation for me isn't that they are always talking and arguing, it's more a level of engagement ... to equate participation with talking out loud doesn't work for me." Another faculty member reacted to these comments, "I agree that it is so hard to gauge participation, rather thoughtful participation. I found what my colleague said to be very interesting; to allow people to write a reflection as opposed to verbal participation. I had never thought of that and I think that is very interesting.

Group and paired discussions are venues that encourage reflection. It was evident, based on the discussions they were having with their colleagues, that faculty were reflecting on their own classroom practices.

The event was not directly observed, therefore *it could only be identified by the faculty member requesting the feedback*; this is considered the first characteristic of this tool. In addition, feedback among colleagues tends not to be evaluative in nature; rather, it is *informative*, with no expectation to account for current and future practices. Most likely, it is informative due to lack of direct observation. A third characteristic of using this tool is that it *allows for more than one individual to receive feedback*. The feedback can be reciprocal or group focused. This characteristic inadvertently creates yet a fourth characteristic, that of *diversity*; the more individuals participating in the reflective process, the more opportunity for different perspectives to exist. Finally, because the event is defined by the individual requesting the feedback and it is not directly observed by the individual giving the feedback, *less accountability* to change the event exists.

Tool 2: Peer Feedback, Event Directly Observed

Another type of peer feedback that exists as a tool for reflection is feedback when the event is directly observed by the individual giving feedback. A colleague providing feedback who observed the event directly can help define the event. A specific example that we came across during our research occurred often during classroom observations. The individual, who was asked to provide feedback, noticed *events* in which there was a lot of freedom given to the students by their instructor. The instructor admitted that allowing such freedom resulted in ultimately not incorporating all the students into a structured lesson. The instructor viewed this as a weakness. Another observation was that one of the instructors failed to have objectives for many of the lessons. This feedback was expressed in an after-class reflection in which the instructor responded, "I wasn't so sure what I wanted them to do as a result of this lesson."

The peer observation helped this faculty member see that some of the teaching practices were of concern and needed to be adjusted, e.g., providing a bit more structure for the students and having objectives for lessons. Another faculty member commented on this tool stating, "Peer feedback provides another avenue for reflection. Getting another colleague's take on my teaching helps me to grow as an instructor."

A characteristic of this tool is that the individual providing the feedback *tends to identify the event (event)*. Additionally, the *feedback tends to be limited. It is provided only by the observer to the person being observed*. One might make the assumption that this reflective tool provides *less opportunity for diversity of opinion* because, typically, only one individual is observing the practice. There is less diversity of opinion due to the limited number of individuals participating in the reflective process.

A fourth characteristic is that direct observation allows for reference to *specifics/examples from the actual observation*. Having the capability to refer to specifics/examples may be necessary if validating the accuracy of the event identified and the feedback given is important to those involved in the process.

Finally, this tool tends to be *more evaluative*—the willingness of faculty members to be evaluative may be the result of direct observation of their peer. Direct observation may provide the reassurance to be more evaluative with the feedback because the observer has *first-hand experience* with the event in question. Overall, this direct observation of an event provides for *accountability* of the feedback.

Tool 3: Journaling

As previously mentioned, one of the most common tools for reflection is journaling. One faculty member stated,

> A technique that I have found to be quite helpful is to try to do a written, daily recap of each class that I teach … I keep a folder labeled "next time" for each of the courses I teach. I put notes into the folder about ideas to try next time, as I'm teaching the course.

Another faculty member described a form of journaling that he uses, "Reflection is a process of examining change and self-regulation. I have used professional development plans, self-studies, and my dissertation to examine my practice."

A characteristic of this tool is the *private nature* of it. When the reflection is private the feedback is *limited to one interpretation*, that of the individual reflecting. In addition, *less diversity or perspective* exists simply due to the feedback being generated by one individual, the individual who is journaling. Fourth, documenting the reflection in writing provides the option of *referring back* to the reflection, and in turn, *making revisions*. It is uncertain as to whether or not the use of journaling facilitates more honest feedback due to a lack of audience or if the feedback can be distorted due to less and/or no accountability to an outside source. That being said, we believe a final characteristic is that journaling facilitates *more honest feedback* due to a lack of audience but the lack of accountability may lessen the likelihood of changed practice.

Tool 4: Student Input

College faculty indicated that student input, in its varied forms, was a reflective tool. One faculty member stated, "Student comments are very important. I learn a great deal from student evaluations as well as direct comments from the students." Another faculty member stated, "I also reflect on my teaching when I view student products, their evaluations and student course evaluations." Yet another faculty member said, "I have never been comfortable being videotaped or being watched by a colleague so I don't do this anymore than I have to. The main tool I use is student feedback."

It is apparent that student evaluations administered at the end of a course are the most common form of student input. This feedback is typically provided anonymously by each student. Although the instructor is not allowed to view the evaluations until the course has officially ended, *authenticity of the feedback* is questioned because some students believe their evaluation of the instructor may impact their grade. Another characteristic of this tool is the numerous students completing the evaluations; this provides an *enormous amount of diversity* in the feedback provided to the instructor. Similar to that of direct observation peer feedback, students can *include specifics or examples* from the class as part of the input the faculty reflect upon. Last, although the student evaluations are completed in a written format and can be used as future references, the instructor is *limited to the written results* of the evaluation; they lack the benefit of asking students what they meant by their comments or to initiate a dialogue centered on student evaluation results.

Tool 5: Shared Research Though Conference Presentations and Publications

Shared research, through conference presentations or publications, was viewed by some faculty as a way to facilitate reflection. Although this tool was not referred to as often as the other tools, one faculty member said, "Reflection means thinking in an evaluative way about one's practice and making a plan to improve. Tools I use include reviewer comments on articles, and paper proposals, reading research and attending conferences." This tool is similar to peer feedback; however, the feedback is in written form.

A characteristic of shared research is the value placed on *feedback being external—outside the affiliated institution*. In addition, because the information collected during this reflective process tends to extend beyond one's affiliated institution, such as, colleagues from other institutions and/or the general educational community, it allows for *much diversity* to exist. Certainly, due to diversity, there is opportunity *for difference of opinion in feedback*. Last, gaining "external" feedback might suggest *less commitment to the defined event*. If the event is not meaningful or important to that particular constituent(s), then the commitment for well-thought-out feedback may not exist, leaving the feedback superficial.

CHOOSING A TOOL: IMPLICATIONS FOR PRACTICE

There are many tools available to individuals who are looking for a way to facilitate reflection. Knowing that journaling is not the only way to facilitate reflection, it is our hope that professionals are open to trying these different tools as they work through the event path. The tools mentioned in detail in this chapter are not the only tools that exist but rather were

Table 7.1.   Reflective Tools and Characteristics

Tools	*Characteristics*
Peer feedback, not directly observed	• Event identified by individual requesting feedback (FB) • More than one person can receive FB, reciprocal and/or group • Diverse opinion due to more individuals providing FB • Larger groups may create reservation and/or less accountability among individuals • Evaluative • Interpretive due to lack of observation
Peer feedback, directly observed	• Event identified by individual giving FB • Typically limited to one person providing FB to another (due to observing) • Can provide specifics/examples from actual observation. • Evaluative • Accountability is strong due to first-hand experience of the event • Accuracy • Less diverse opinion
Journaling	• Private • Limited to one interpretation • Documented in writing, option of referring back • Can be more honest due to lack of audience • Can be revised
Student input	• Authenticity is questioned • Different perspective due to different role • Written format, unable to gain clarification from student • Diverse opinion • Confidential • Can provide specifics/examples due to participation in class
Research-conferences, publications	• Data driven FB • Extends beyond inner circle, that is, colleagues at same institution • Diverse opinion • May lack commitment due to not knowing individual providing FB to

the ones mentioned by participants in our studies. We encourage professionals to search out additional tools to encourage the reflective process.

In deciding which tool to use, we recommend considering the source of the feedback, that is, is it first person or second person? If you're reflecting on your own events, you may choose to use journaling as a tool. However, if someone else is reflecting on your event, the more appropriate tool may be a formal peer evaluation. Also, be attentive to the *means* by which the information is being recorded. The information collected comes from someone, either the person trying to reflect, or someone directly or indirectly involved in that person's life, and this human aspect of the tool can influence the epistemic weight of the information. In other words, the tool provides the information and the question then becomes, to what extent does the person trying to reflect place value on the information provided by the tool. Does this person believe the information is credible? Are they placing value on the information? These questions need to be considered as we make the argument that the appropriate tool will likely contribute to a successful reflection.

It is reasonable to think that all professionals could benefit from making use of these tools. If professionals do not use tools to collect accurate and pertinent information, they will be limiting their reflective process. As professionals continue to mull over how certain tools promote reflection and develop professionally, consider these questions or suggestions:

1. Tools help organize or structure our reflection process; not using such tools may result in a feeling of disorganization, chaos with our thoughts (cognition) (Wlodarsky & Walters, 2006). These tools should be viewed as a resource, not a burden to the reflective process (Wlodarsky & Walters, 2007).

2. What tool(s) are most appropriate to the event of practice or the practice context? As each reflection is unique based on the event, certain tools may be more suitable for certain contexts. For example, the use of student input, as a means to reflect on one's writing for publication, is probably of limited value. Typically, faculty would look to their peers or research to provide feedback on the writing(s) they reflect upon, which seems more appropriate. Another example would be a confrontation between a student and faculty member. Most likely, one couldn't use the peer feedback direct observation tool, simply because their colleague probably wasn't present to directly observe the confrontation. Rather, it would seem more appropriate for a faculty member to use feedback from a peer who didn't directly observe the event, and/or journaling as a tool to reflect on the event, in this case, the confrontation.

3. As mentioned previously, findings suggest that reflection can lead to changes in practice. Although, in some cases, the influence in terms of change may be minimal, reflection certainly facilitated some change. Often, change occurs in small increments, and can be more effective when approached in this manner. Although minimal, change due to reflection should not be devalued (Ferry & Ross-Gordon, 1998; Hoffman-Kipp, Artiles, & Lopez-Torres, 2003; Schön, 1987).

4. If change does not occur, a sense of awareness that may not have existed prior to working through the process is most likely to be present. Obviously, in order for a behavior change to take place, awareness through reflection needs to take place. Simply having awareness of an event should not be diminished, as this awareness may lead to the realization of satisfaction with or tolerance of the existing event, or may lead to future change in practice.

CONCLUSION

We have confirmed that various methods are available to promote reflection and encourage professionals to become critical consumers of research, participants in research discussions, and developers of research-based classroom decision making (Cochran-Smith & Lytle, 1992; Zeichner, 1994). Using the tools outlined in this chapter, or other tools to facilitate the reflective process is to embrace a culture of continually improving oneself and the environment in which one interacts professionally.

QUESTIONS FOR INDIVIDUAL, GROUP, OR ORGANIZATIONAL FOLLOW-UP AND/OR CONSIDERATION

1. Determine the event of practice or practice context that you want to reflect on.

2. What tool(s) are most appropriate to this event of practice or the practice context?

3. Refer to the event path chapter for specifics of walking yourself through the event path with the appropriate tool(s).

4. Understand, in some cases, the influence in terms of change may be minimal therefore set realistic expectations for the reflective process.

5. If no change has occurred, do not automatically assume it has to do with the tool being used, rather, awareness may simply have developed which is a part of the overall reflective process or it may be a sign of confirmation that the event that took place is actually working and therefore change does not need to occur.

6. If awareness is not enough and/or change is minimal, consider using a different tool to facilitate the reflective process. Often professionals think they know what tool will best serve them and they may be mistaken.

CHAPTER 8

CHANGE

On a crisp fall morning, at the midpoint of his career as an associate professor, tracking beautifully toward full professor, Alexander Eggen, fresh cup of coffee in hand, was preoccupied with a more than serious set of e-mails from his dean. The college of education, as was true of most similar institutions across the country, had ridden the "cash cow" of its MEd program for nearly 2 decades. Never able, politically, to work through the weeds of merit pay for teachers, state boards' of education had used the attainment of higher degrees as an objective criterion on which to base step-raises and salary decisions. The resultant rush to create MEd programs had created a more-than-cottage industry in higher education. Colleges of education across the state and nation generated hundreds of millions in tuition revenue annually—and in many cases on the backs of nontenured, adjunct professional faculty at minimal cost to the institutions.

All was well in the ivory tower until their own particular state, responding to a variety of pressures, backed away from the MEd in its licensure programs. And for better or worse, for right or for wrong, it was now "for richer, for poorer" for colleges of education across the state. The MEd rug had been pulled out from under higher education's collective and individual cash flows and everyone was panicked.

Eggen's college dean, in a rehearsal of a similar e-mail she had received from her provost the night before, was explaining a series of painful budget cuts to manage the 21% enrollment decline in MEd programs from the previous academic year. The second e-mail from the dean invited Eggen to the dean's suite for a 2 P.M. meeting.

"You've got to be kidding!" slipped through Eggen's lips before he could self-edit. His dean had just explained that he was being released from half his teaching

Reflection and the College Teacher: A Solution for Higher Education
pp. 93–107
Copyright © 2014 by Information Age Publishing
All rights of reproduction in any form reserved.

assignments for the remainder of the academic year, in order to pursue a partner-ship with a large, urban school district in the state. The goal of the new partnership was clear: identifying and creating an innovative, nondegree-based credential for education professionals on a turnaround time that was unheard of for higher edu-cation: three months. And ideally, meeting the goal would also create enhanced rev-enue for the university to offset declines in the degree programs. The irony of all of this did not escape Eggen, who had fought for, and finally given up on, this type of systemic change in his college for a decade: change would now come, potentially mean and hard, and driven from factors outside the control of the institution. But change nevertheless.

THE LITERATURE OF REFLECTION AND CHANGE

As long as there have been human institutions, there have been struggles to create and monitor change in those institutions. The process of institu-tionalization carries with it an implied process of developing policies and procedures to organize institutional activities. These drive the formation of gatekeepers, rule makers, and enforcers who monitor these policies and procedures, hence the emergence of the bureaucratic classes. As Ken-neth Galbraith and others have observed: those who have power are loathe to give up that power. Consequently, most institutions are essen-tially conservative in the traditional meaning of that term. Conservative in that they develop a manner of doing things, and then prefer, over time, their own manner of doing things above any other way. Institutions are thus self-perpetuating and resistant to those who, in Kouzes and Posner's (2007) terms, *challenge the system*. In the preface to this important and oft-used text, these authors write:

> there are no shortages of challenging opportunities (in organizations). In these extraordinary times, the challenges seem only to be increasing in number and complexity. All generations confront their own serious threats and receive their own favorable circumstances. The abundance of chal-lenges is not the issue. It's how we respond to them that matters. Through our responses to challenges, we all have the potential to seriously worsen or profoundly improve the world in which we live and work. (p. xi)

At the core of all of this discussion of challenge and opportunity, threats and circumstances, is the issue of *change*. In the story that leads this chapter, the issue of change relates to a number of key stakeholders. The professor: can he rise above the parochial interests of his individual research and teaching interests? The college: can it grow beyond its his-toric dependence upon a single, comfortable degree toward innovative and entrepreneurial invention? The broader faculty: can they get behind the creative engagement of a colleague in potentially a bold, creative and structural movement? *Change*. If history and literature is any guide, and it usually is, at the interface between old and new, tried and innovative, conservative and creative, the institutions and individuals who embrace change first will have the greatest opportunities to realize and capture the benefits of growth in the emergent future. Those who resist change are likely not to survive.

As we explored the process of reflection for our study group in the original research, we saw a consistent focus on change that emerged, unsolicited, from participants across all experience levels of the professors we worked with. For novice and expert alike, the most common descriptions of reflection on practice linked the past experience and the information carried forward journals, evaluations, student comments, peer reviews to a conscious decision to do something different; to change.

CHANGE AS INNOVATION

One of the seminal texts on change in many people's estimations is E.M. Rogers' *Diffusion of Innovations* (2003), now in its fifth edition since it was first published in 1962. Rogers defined diffusion as,

> one part of a larger process which begins with a perceived problem or need, through research and development on a possible solution, the decision by a change agency that this innovation should be diffused, and then its diffusion (leading to certain consequences). (p. xvi)

Comparing this definition of diffusion, developed in a sociological field in the early 1960s, to our model of reflective decision making, we see a high degree of similarity between the two: each begin with a problem or precipitating event; each have a cognition stage wherein knowledge is evaluated, synthesized, and applied. Rogers' uses research and development, we simply say cognition; each involves a decision-making actor or agent; each involves a decision to either change (or adopt a new practice) or not to change. The questions for us, and for Rogers, involve what conditions optimize the possibility that change actually occurs. Rogers (2003) concluded several things:

> for most individuals, one means of coping with the inherent uncertainty about an innovation's consequences is to try out the new idea on a partial basis ... most individuals will not adopt an innovation without trying it first on a probationary basis. (p. 172)

Second, individuals may be more likely to adopt a new practice if it can be broken down into pieces or "trial sized portions" and tried briefly or for short periods. Third, Rogers observed that for some individuals and for some innovations the trial of a new idea by a peer like themselves can substitute, at least in part, for their own trial of an innovation. This "trial by others" provides a kind of vicarious trial for an individual. (p. 172)

These ideas, such as trial in a short-term cycle testing scenario, peer input, and selective piloting, all have their counterparts in modern education practices and reform efforts.

THE CONTINUING STRUGGLE FOR DEFINITIONS

An important addition to the literature of reflection and reflective practice was published in a comprehensive review of the literature of reflective processes. In particular as it concerns this chapter, the focus in this literature review was to identify the various ways in which reflective practices have been observed and discussed in the context of particular education programs or projects. From their view, they were interested in the instrumental uses of reflective practice: was reflection in any of its various definitions treated in the literature as causal of professional development, individually or with cohorts of practitioners? And if or when reflective practice was viewed as an essential tool to create change in individual educators or in groups of educators, was their evidence that this change, in fact, occurred (Kahn et al., 2008)?

In their path toward answering these questions, Kahn et al. covered similar ground as we have: much ambiguity exists in the basic definition of reflection or reflective practice; much variety exists in the observable behaviors that pass for reflection; and much work remains to both clearly define the idea and then to measure it, describe it, and ground it in practice. Kahn et al. further observed, as with Clegg, Tan, and Saeidi (2002) that "reflection essentially is used as a metaphor for problematizing professional practice" (p. 4), or reflection for some is nothing more than "thinking about what happened yesterday." Springing from this definitional ambiguity, Kahn et al. cataloged a broad collection of research focused on reflection, reflective practice, or critical reflection. Their goal in part was to identify whether such practices resulted in professional development, for example, positive changes in professional behavior, for individuals and cohorts. They further specified that the behaviors of interest included: "enhanced capacity for practice, ability to engage in specific accessible reflective processes, and an ability to engage in, become aware of, or understand aspects of practice" (p. 166).

Ultimately, Kahn et al. (2008) determined that "while changes may be evident in practice, it is clear that when entire cohorts are considered, there is significant variation for individual members of staff, ranging from little to extensive change in practice." They continued,

Indeed, the most commonly identified outcomes in the main sample [of the literature studied in this meta-analysis] also concerned changes in practice and the ability to engage in specific reflective processes, with changes in personal qualities or professional identity seen far less frequently. (p. 168)

In reviewing, finally, the body of literature they studied, Kahn et al. (2008) came to a rather stark, but not necessarily unanticipated conclusion with respect to the outcomes of grand-scale education efforts:

Terms such as "reflection" or "reflective practice" were, however, only rarely unpacked within the documentation. While exploration of their meaning might well occur during a program, it was clear in the documentation that the ability to engage in a reflective process was not simply an end in itself. Other intended outcomes flowing from the application of reflective processes included the ability to innovate, the willingness to take risks, a framework for career-long development and so on. A direct link was made in each program between reflective processes and professional development, with the use of reflection to support self-improvement and adaptation of practice prevalent to varying extents, as with one program which sought to promote "a framework for ... career-long development based on reflective practice." This was typically set within a context of change within higher education. (p. 170)

In short, for these authors, the literature surrounding reflective practice was thick with outcomes expectations: education systems adopt the language and "practices" (whatever these have come to mean really) instrumentally. Education institutions and programs encourage, require, or use reflective processes instrumentally to cause change in individuals and among cohorts of practitioners. Yet, as Kahn et al. (2008) observed, actual performance data have been, in many cases, ambiguous or inconclusive as to whether this change really takes place.

We argue at this point and flowing from our research, that reflection or reflective processes, and in our case the event path of reflection at the center of focus in this book, results in change in practice at the individual level if and when a variety of conditions exist to support that change. Nevertheless, we would continue to agree with Kahn et al. and others (Clegg, Tan, & Saeidi, 2002; Lyons, 2006) that the degree or reality of change is highly variable within cohorts of education professionals and even for individuals in problematized contexts.

REFLEXIVITY AND CHANGE: FINDING SELF IN THE PROCESS

A second significant and recent contribution to the literature that moved beyond a single program or research description was that of Wright (2009), who approached the construct of reflection on practice through, again, Schön's work, but added an interesting and unique contribution to the change discussion: the idea of reflexivity. Wright's study was the result of a professional development experience she engaged with while serving as a school principal. The *Reflections on Practice: Institute for School Leaders* program "emphasized personal, collaborative and professional reflection by critically examining theory, questioning assumptions and practices, and conducting action research and participating in onsite/on line workshops" (p. 262).

As a part of this workshop experience, she and other participants were required to maintain participation journals. Wright's journal ultimately became the data for this critical and reflective essay on how principal's effect change in their environments through the use of reflective practices. It is clear from her treatment of reflection that she is fully complicit with the concept of "instrumental reflection" as discussed earlier in this chapter and by others (Clegg, Tan, & Saeidi, 2002; Kahn et al., 2008; Lyons, 2006). Wright (2009) struggled with the moral tension between existing policy environments that she perceives to be limiting her choices as an education administrator, and the results of her reflective efforts that lead her to decisions to change in counterdirections. For Wright, she returned to Schön's "reflection as decision making in a swamp" of difficult and overwhelming choices, and to Wilson's (2008) use of reflection-on-the-future as "imagining or reflecting on what might be possible ... to develop operational strategies which hopefully will deliver concrete reality" (p. 179). Importantly, Wright formed a conclusion that foregrounds *change*:

> I came to understand that if individual change is to be a precursor to collective change, reflection should involve the interruption of taken-for-granted behavioral patterns and unexamined assumptions that perpetuate the status quo. When long-standing norms are interrupted, practitioners engage in second-order change that has potential for transformational or behavioral change ... consequently, the practitioner's identity is fluid and evolves. (p. 263)

To find the power or efficacy to "disrupt the taken-for-granted behaviors," Wright addresses herself to the distinction, attributed to Fendler (2003), that *reflexion* is differentiated from *reflection*. "Reflexivity disrupts habituated patterns of thinking and interrogates beliefs and practices particularly around internalized structures and preoccupations based on one's position of power and privilege (Foster, 1986)." Wright (2009) then continues from her own journal:

> Reflexivity involves being vulnerable to exposing, challenging and disrupting thinking and practice by openly questioning the extent to which our

decisions and actions are value-laden. When principals practice reflexivity, they consciously take responsibility for their actions and the impact on others and school improvement efforts. (p. 17)

Wright distinguished reflexivity as an element in effective reflection, part of the cognitive consideration of information, but characterized as the intentional questioning of self: of identity, of behavior, of values, of choices. She added, finally, a helpful qualification to the definition of reflection: "Reflection is metaphor for learning in the swamp. This continuous reinterpretation of that which we perceive as already understanding makes reflection stand apart from mere thoughtfulness (p. 266)."

GREGOIRE'S COGNITIVE-AFFECTIVE CONCEPTUAL CHANGE MODEL

Another view of the relationship between reflection and change is provided in an evaluation study of Gregoire's (2003) *cognitive-affective conceptual change* model for professional development, reported in 2010 (Ebert & Crippen, 2010). The cognitive-affective conceptual change approach to professional development was formed around the professional development activities of a set of mathematics teachers, and evolved into a discussion of conceptual change, which was outlined in flow-chart form (Gregoire, 2003). This theoretical model, applied in practice with great success, emphasized an initial cognitive experience by the participants, termed "presentation of the reform message." This message was essentially an advanced organizer for the teacher that confronted the teacher, as Wilson (2008) advocated, about practice-level behaviors, beliefs, or assumptions regarding their work with students in the classroom prior to the professional development sequence. This advanced messaging could then either be accepted or rejected by the participant. Gregoire found that individuals who accepted an "implication of self" in that message, essentially agreeing with the message, evidenced a greater degree of conceptual and practice change over time. Our treatment of the *event* in Chapter 5 foregrounds the conceptual weight of the precipitating confrontation with reality or real performance that Gregoire discusses.

Ebert and Crippen (2010) replicated the cognitive-affective conceptual change model using science teachers to test the practicality and cross-validity of the model with science teachers. This 2010 study found that the model was successful following the same line of reasoning as the original 2003 study, but these authors centralized the role and relationship of reflective practices to the model more explicitly than the earlier one. Ebert and Crippen further identified an intentional cognitive processing of information from experience and from the advanced messaging in a way that very much supports our findings and use of *cognition* in Chapter 6 of this current text. They borrowed Bransford, Brown, and Cocking's (1999) phrase "semantic restructuring of cognitive resources" (p. 148) to describe the cognitive component of this change model.

Critical for our discussion here, Ebert and Crippen (2010) explicitly identified time to reflect or to engage in a process of reflection as at the heart of successful professional development programs: "Having the opportunity to collaborate, reflect, and receive meaningful feedback from colleagues, and learning to use research-based instruments for reflection, enables teachers to confront deeply held personal beliefs about their practices" (p. 373). Furthermore,

> Inherent in the [cognitive-affective conceptual change model] is the notion that professional development programs occur over time, taking advantage of teacher enactive mastery and providing time and opportunity for practice ... funding agencies and policy makers should provide opportunity for reflection. (p. 376)

CHANGE AND DEFICIENCY

In our research, there was an unmistakable pattern of change that derived from identification and correction of deficiencies in practice on the part of our study sample. The participant responses suggested that as they mentally reviewed a completed class, for example, looked at student work, graded tests, read student or peer evaluations, looking for weaknesses that could be corrected or strengthened. This self-critique or evaluative mindset appeared to drive most decisions to change on the part of our participants. In fact, all but three of the individual path maps that we created in the original study included a specific moment in the life of the individual when the process lead to a change in behavior (in teaching approach, method, or assignment for example) and a new future. This observation supports that of Ebert and Crippen's (2010) use of language such as "confront ... reform ... acknowledge ... and threat." This is the idea that motivation for change, at the individual level, may be best activated when it includes clear information about current or past performance that reveals a level of deficiency. This creates an opportunity to compare current or past performance with alternative futures that are within the decision-making authority of the individual and creates a period of cognitive engagement. Ebert and Crippen's contribution, that our research did not address, is the issue of time. Reflective processes take time, and consequently, as Schon wrote, reflection must reach a level of practiced engagement so that, when the pressures of decision-making-in-the-swamp emerge, the professional defaults to better quality decisions.

Our observation also resonates with Rogers' (2003) acknowledgement of future possibilities and the opportunity for trial, error, and correction in a supportive environment. This is somewhat parallel, again, to Gregoire (2003) and Ebert and Crippen's (2010) use of a reform message, almost as an advanced organizer for what the future should look like, early in the change process, or in our model, an authentic event. It further resonates with Wright's (2009) and Wilson's (2008) use of the language of future orientation for practice change and reflection. For our study sample, their reflections on practice emerged in an environment where deficiency was almost acceptable so long as it was highlighted in a process of reflective change. There was a forgone conclusion (a prewritten reform message, in Gregoire's usage) that a continuous process of critique and growth was necessary in the system, and that future practice should be demonstrably different from past practice. This is, perhaps, a theoretical progressivism operationalized into college practice.

RENEWAL AND CONFIRMATION

Nevertheless, we cannot overlook the fact that for some, reflection is ultimately not entirely a tool for uncovering and rectifying deficiencies in performance or practice, but in fact a process of discovery of strengths and successes, and an opportunity to both celebrate those, and to confirm and plan for continuation in that same path. Three of the maps which emerged for us (see Chapter 4 for a summary of the original *Event Path* research findings) described the reflection path for education professors who made a conscientious attempt to review information about a past experience, generally these were class sessions where they taught some group of students to self-evaluate performance for the purpose of future improvement. In these three cases, after the cognitive process of information review, these professors concluded that they were pleased with their performance, that the event (using our *path* language) had not created tension or displeasure, but had, in final analysis, proven quite satisfying.

For these professors, change, rejecting and abandoning past practice in favor of a different future, would be abandoning past success in favor of an unknown. They held evidence that their past performance was worth repeating: positive student evaluations, reinforcing peer reviews, examples of student work that demonstrated that the students had learned well the concepts being taught. These professors found confirmatory evidence that the structural elements or characteristics of the event that they had both created and experienced fully met their individual goals.

INTERRUPTING BEHAVIORS FOR A REIMAGINED FUTURE

Our research participants, as judged from the stories and examples that they provided us, would resonate with two key ideas that emerge from the recent literature of reflection and change. They seemed to be most influenced in their reflections and in their future planning for change by a confrontation with a behavioral deficiency. Their behavior was interrupted by an observation that they were not functioning optimally so as to fully perform to a level of satisfaction. There were a variety of ways in which this behavior interruption occurred. For some, it was reading student evaluations. For others, it was hearing from a peer either directly or in a written observation report. Yet others reported that they synthesized this conclusion after looking at student performance on tests and written papers. One professor wrote,

> A technique that I have found quite helpful is to try to do a written daily recap of each class that I teach. Sometimes the recap is quite brief; other days it may be somewhat detailed. When I teach the course again, I can refer to these daily recaps to reflect upon changes that need to be made.

Yet another professor wrote, *"I define reflection as focused thinking about my teaching. I do this informally after each class by asking myself what went well, what didn't go as well and what I might change in the future."* These professors, in these same narrative responses, shared stories about "replaying the events of the class in my head as I drove home after class." Another professor wrote, *"I am really bothered when a class ends and I know it didn't work like I know it should have ... I dwell on this for days, and I usually end up talking to two other professors about what happened in the class."*

These professors had their movement through time interrupted by an event that was disconsonant with an idealized view of reality or worded differently, by performance expectations. Critically for us, we observe that nearly all of our study subjects identified an objectified information or data source, that is, evaluations, written comments, student work samples, peer reviews. They also identify a cognitive path where they process or revisit the event through the lens of these data, and then reimagine a future that evolves along a different performance pathway. This is, as Wright (2009) wrote, a "best example" use of reflective and reflexive thinking: realizing that what we thought we knew about ourselves, in this case teaching performance, was not true and needed revision and revisiting. This confrontation with self, or interruption of behavior, seems critical for realizing change through reflection, and seems thus to be inseparable from the reflective pathway.

The second key idea emerging from the literature that is directly observable in our participants, and thus a part of our reflective path, is the idea from Rogers (2003) and Wilson (2008) of the reimagined future. The aphorism that "if you always do what you've always done, you will always get the same results" is quite true in education. Yet many colleges seem hidebound and impervious to imagining a future that is outside the box of their past accomplishments. In a different text, Kouzes and Posner (2010) wrote that focusing on the future remains one of the highest and distinctive characteristics of leadership:

> The capacity to imagine and articulate exciting future possibilities is the defining competence of leaders. Leaders are custodians of the future. They are concerned about tomorrow's world and those who will inherit it. They ask, "What's new? What's next? What's going to happen after the current project is completed?" They think beyond what's directly in front of them, peer into the distance, imagine what's over the horizon, and move forward toward a new and compelling future. (p. 46)

The process of change through reflection is, in the most profound and authentic sense, learning to be a leader of one's own professional and personal self. To escape the bonds of the past and past performance mistakes, miscalculations, and miscues, and reimagine a future where one actively performs in a different way, toward a different goal or end, through a different means, or in a different method.

Our participants determined to reach a different outcome "the next time" the class was taught, or the manuscript was submitted, or the interpersonal encounter was repeated. One professor wrote: "*I look back on lessons, presentations and other pieces of work for ways to improve teaching and gain knowledge and suggestions for future lessons.*" Another professor wrote, "*reflection is self-examination ... examining different aspects of your professional behavior and addressing areas that need improvement.*" For these and other professors, reflection produced a conscious and identifiable moment of choice: I will not allow the next event to obtain the same outcomes as the last one.

THE BENEFITS OF REFLECTION ON CHANGE

So, confronting and interrupting existing performance to insert an evolved and changed vision of the future, and then acting to see that future materialized. *Change*. Whether one accepts change gracefully, or fights it, it is a given in professional fields. Many of us, perhaps because of disposition or personality, embrace change. We relish a rapid pace of movement around and about the status quo. For us, boredom sets in when we are too often confronted with stasis in our professional lives. For others, change is fraught with emotional tension. It is difficult. It is stressful in a negative way and it is, consequently, resisted. But again, as history shows, it is inevitable. Among other reasons change is necessitated:

1. to improve on past deficiencies;
2. to solidify and reinforce past successes;
3. to manage changing contingencies, and consequently is also driven by timetables not of our choosing; and
4. to find a consensus or center for sociocultural compromise.

In all of these circumstances, we find that a reflective approach to change protects the individual and the organization from repeating the mistakes of the past in the unrealized future that Wilson (2008) and Rogers (2003) wrote about. Reflection, as demonstrated in the event path at the core of this book, is a process that can lead to change, but which connects past practice and experience to the unrealized future in an informed manner. The information collected through the tools of reflection, processed cognitively in a way that leads to informed possible futures from which to select trial pathways, guards the professional against thoughtless, reactionary, and fad-driven pivots into a future that is in no way preferable to the past.

CONDITIONS WHICH SUPPORT AND INHIBIT CHANGE

In the final analysis, it seems clear to us that change can and does emerge from a systematic implementation of a process of reflective analysis by individuals and in institutions. Although this process is not guaranteed to produce change, it seems that there are conditions in which the process is more conducive to producing change than others. From the literature and from our careful consideration of the data we've collected over the years of our study, we would note and discuss briefly three criteria or situations wherein change is more likely to occur than otherwise.

First, regardless of the terminology one incorporates for the precipitating event that triggers the reflection process it seems clear that interrupting past practices in a way that is knowable, meaningful, and truly disrupting to the individual or organization seems requisite to change. This implies that change is very related to the degree to which present practices are monitored, documented, and described. Lacking informed feedback, through some type of authentic and realistic assessment framework, blinds the individual and the institution to the current "state of practice." This blindness translates to an inability to experience the inter-ruption necessary to know that change is needed. Lacking any means of meaningful confrontation that, following Wright (2009), "what you know about yourself is not true," certainly discounts the potential for meaning-ful change. If you are not looking realistically at present performance, you have no capacity to triangulate or refine future performance; no capacity for reimagining a future that is different because "different from what" is unanswerable.

Second, the potential for change seems highly related to how firmly the individual or the institution holds to its identity. Is identity fixed or is it fluid? Does the individual professor perceive that he or she has "arrived" fully, with an unquestioned satisfaction, and no space for move-ment? Am I all that I can be, or is growth possible? Is the college fully expanded strategically to fill all of the available niche space or are there unmet and unattained vistas still to be explored? As much as anything, these questions reflect and reveal disposition for change, something that we and others discussed early on in this book. Some individuals seem pre-disposed or hardwired to constantly seek change. Some individuals seem not to be. Some colleges seem satisfied and complacent to live within the boundaries that their histories have evolved and endorsed. Some do not. Beyond this dispositional dynamism, further related to the question of identity and change is the influence of external structures, meta-narra-tives, and hegemonies on the potential for change. Our college of educa-tion has historically existed as a provider of licenses for the K-12 education community. Nearly a decade ago, it added a doctoral program in leadership studies that has, periodically, admitted students that are not from historic K-12 backgrounds. Recently, we have renamed one of our departments to include the conceptual ideas of "informal and community education," thereby endorsing and fostering a conversation about the broader concerns of teaching and learning outside of and beyond K-12 education and licensure. The most immediate potential change out of this conversation is a working white paper on a master's degree in adult edu-cation, with an emphasis in community and informal education that is likely to now be a reimagined future in the college. Nevertheless, these discussions have languished without deeply held criticisms from respected colleagues who remain rooted in a vision for the identity of our college as a K-12 oriented college of education. Hence, these unheard voices are influencing and challenging the process of identity change in our college.

Third and finally, it seems that change is more likely to emerge at the end of the reflection process where an attitude of vulnerability for individ-ual professors and for the college is protected, supported in practice, and fostered. Can the individual admit to deficiencies in performance without becoming the target of supervisory and collegial disdain? Is there an attitude, driven from ego or from fear, that the individual and the college itself must, at all costs, present herself or itself as fundamentally "perfected" in ability or capability? We are speaking to personal and institutional ego directly at this point. Culturally, no single group of professionals, perhaps other than medical doctors, have crafted, inculcated, and disseminated strength of ego more profoundly than college professors. We are, by default in our culture, "the" source of information, "the" experts. For us individually or corporately to believe our own media too strongly is to blind us to the real need to change in ways that evolve instructional methods, research methods, key questions for inquiry, and which capture the myriad, fine details of our role, function, and responsibilities in society and in our fields of inquiry and practice. Change emerges best out of chastened confidence. Confidence, certainly, that we are strategically important as gatekeepers to practice and as researchers of teaching and learning. But confidence that is always subject to revisions, to improvements, to refinement, to *change*.

QUESTIONS FOR INDIVIDUAL FOLLOW-UP

1. As a professor, how confident do you feel that you can share a felt professional or personal weakness with your department chair, with your dean, or with a trusted colleague, and receive support for improvement in that area without penalty?

2. Does your college evaluation system or, Promotion and Tenure allow or encourage you to document areas where you have reason to believe you need to improve? Is there informal pressure to "hedge" in these processes, or do you fully believe you can or should be honest with these processes? If you feel pressure to "hide" performance deficiencies do you believe this is healthy for you or your college, and how might you move this situation toward a healthier and more change-conducive environment?

3. Do you systematically collect information about your performance (perhaps using one of the tools we discussed in Chapter 7) that has the potentially to honestly confront and disrupt your practices? What strength of information would it take to truly disrupt your continuation of past practices?

QUESTIONS FOR GROUP OR ORGANIZATIONAL CONSIDERATION

1. How does the assessment system utilized in the college provide sufficiently explicit description of professional practices and accom-

plishments such that the assessment system confronts and disrupts practices where that is necessary? Be honest: is the system designed for objective honesty, or to sustain a historic view that the system is "fixed" and final?

2. Are faculty and staff encouraged to honestly critique and improve on past performance? How is self-critique incentivized in faculty and staff evaluation systems?

3. Are there programs in place to help faculty and staff change and improve when they choose to do this? If a faculty member, for example, wanted to learn new instructional methods or to incorporate technology in instruction differently, are their support scaffolds in the college or university to assist?

4. What professional niches, outside of "what you have always done" require the same knowledge domains and/or practice skills, offer you the opportunity for change and growth? Do you perceive growth primarily as "growing the enrollment of the same kind of programs and students" or "growing the number of types of programs and kinds of students?"

CHAPTER 9

THE REFLECTIVE COLLEGE OF EDUCATION

PART 1: MACROLEVEL

As we come to the end of our treatment of reflection by or among teacher educators, and in the college of education setting within the university, it seems important to push the conversation full circle, back to the societal and external concerns that are currently grating against the existence, in some situations, of colleges of education and education faculty members individually. Our research, as outlined, presented, and summarized across this text, describes an event-path model for professional reflection that affords the individual faculty member or the college, as a unit, the tools and methods necessary to move from a professional or personal event in a thoughtful and strategic manner toward innovative and enhanced performance. This innovation can be observed, and has been, at the individual level, as we have described individual professors in a college of education that have worked to improve their teaching, research, and service.

To a far lesser extent, unfortunately, have we seen these individualized practices incorporated in a systematic way across the width and breadth of entire colleges. Indeed, the literature surrounding reflection, as we've discussed in earlier chapters, suggests that this jump from the individual faculty member, to the unit, or in intentional ways to more effectively link the college to its broader society, are badly lacking in higher education in the United States. It seems critical then, that we take this final chapter to conceptualize and discuss a model for systematizing professional reflection along this continuum, as illustrated in Figure 9.1.

Reflection and the College Teacher: A Solution for Higher Education
pp. 109–122
Copyright © 2014 by Information Age Publishing

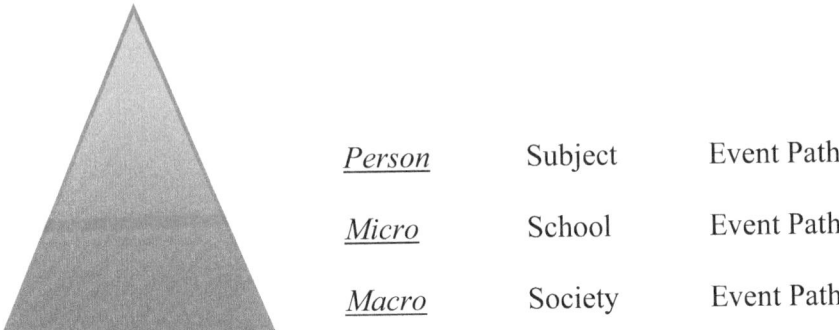

Person	Subject	Event Path
Micro	School	Event Path
Macro	Society	Event Path

Figure 9.1.   A person-micro-macro application of professional reflection using the event path model.

As Illustrated in Figure 9.1, a systematized model of professional reflection using the event path should and will, to be effective, incorporate individual professors (person), the college as a unit (microlevel) and links to societal expectations, concerns, and needs (macrolevel). Unfortunately, limitations in the use of a reflection model systematically result in diminished effectiveness of individual professors, diminished effectiveness and innovation in colleges, and a failure to react to societal trends effectively in the college, or a failure of colleges to more effectively influence and shape the education conversations in society. We are too frequently, reduced to reactive thinking and decision making, and too infrequently masters of our own destinies, actively shaping our professional worlds.

Looking at these three levels in reverse order, working up the pyramid from Figure 9.1, it is possible to consider how systematic application of the event path reflection model can inform and empower colleges of education at the macro, or societal level. In engaging this conversation, we would like to revisit the pressures on colleges of education that we initially discussed in Chapter 1 of the text. Our comments and discussion are in some cases questions without answers, perhaps the best type of questions, requiring open-ended thought. In some cases, we also suggest strategies, share case examples of both success and failure, but always pushing toward systemic and systematic utilization of reflection as a key indicator of eventual progress.

Social Conceptions

As we finish this manuscript, the nation is apparently at war with higher education institutions. In our local newspaper this morning, there were three "wire reports" on the "outrageous" costs to students of obtaining college degrees, the "horrendous" debt loads that graduates are carrying, and the "drag on the overall economy" of student loans. Regardless of individual opinions on the various sides of these debates, clearly colleges must reflect on, and develop reasonable responses to, these discussions and attacks.

Are colleges providing value to students commensurate with the economic costs of obtaining the degree? This is the question coming at colleges from across a spectrum of critique, not only from historically antagonistic corners, but increasingly from historic supporters of higher learning efforts. At our private university, what do we do for education students that is worth an additional $100,000 in tuition over and above the tuition of a state institution, particularly when the degrees and curriculum are tied to licenses such that we deliver the same courses? Without a substantive answer to these questions, in times of national economic decline, it becomes problematic to continue to justify (particularly in expensive private universities) the high level of tuition attached to degrees for entry into lower salaried fields. Colleges must reflect on the relationship between their costs to students and the value of the services and degrees provided. Absent well-reasoned and reflective explanations, the college is ill prepared to respond to such social critiques.

Working through a systematic application of the event path model, we should identify appropriate data to inform discussions of the relative costs of our programs. What are the longer term impacts of debt to our students? Are there delivery models and schedules for coursework and degrees that could minimize the time to complete a degree? Can we provide initial licensure in 3 years by utilizing summer terms, and if so, how do we create field experiences during summer months when most K-12 schools are out of session? What is the relationship between sequences of coursework and professional competence? Can the professional school curriculum be thinned out without compromising the expertise of graduates? What is the continuum between initial licensure, professional development, and career ladders? These questions and many others should drive regular conversations in colleges of education. We are at a point of change in our institutions and society, and colleges that fail to address these fundamental societal pressures will ultimately lose the debates.

Philosophic Tensions

As we stated in Chapter 1, how do we triangulate a position that rejects overly narrow assumptions and generalizations on both ends of the political spectrum, taking the high road of academic excellence, intellectual honesty, and ethical practice that centralizes social good for all of our citizens? Colleges must reflect on the balance between their essences as academic programs versus clinical or professional license programs. In that vein, we must also reflect and resolve the ongoing struggles for individual faculty to situate themselves on the continuum of research scholars and clinical practitioners.

What are the distinctive differences between a professional school and a traditional college? In our own college, we have experienced a decades long struggle to answer this question, and in ways that have profoundly impacted and shaped our own careers. As we have served on hiring committees for new colleagues, for example, we have engaged in debates and heated conversations regarding appropriate qualifications and credentials for education faculty. Do we want colleagues who are "freshly minted doctors" with little or no work experience in K-12 practice but who are "up on" research methods, theory, and literature? Do we want experienced classroom teachers who have demonstrated effective practice, and have incidentally earned their doctorates? Whether this dichotomy is real or imagined, we have a sense that it is a cultural struggle playing out in more than just our own college. How can we reject what we believe to be a false dichotomy toward a more nuanced, enlightened and substantive balancing of both areas? We share this one struggle as only one idea of the philosophical tension facing colleges of education.

A second area of philosophical tension that is likely facing colleges of education is the typical imbalance within these organizations toward K-12 practice. Although K-12 education is historically a large emphasis of colleges of education, clearly teaching and learning occur in society in much different, and even larger arenas than K-12. Demographically, K-12 education is shrinking in the United States, and is likely to continue to do so for generations. The baby boomer population, that group of 75 million adults whose children populated the K-12 growth years, are now beyond child-bearing years. Successive generations are now smaller and having fewer children. The trend line is thus moving in a negative growth direction for K-12. The large and numerous colleges of education that grew into the demographic space afforded by the baby boom years will shrink with the demographic trend line if they fail to reconceptualize and repurpose their skills, knowledge, and faculties toward adult education in its various conceptions, from workforce development, adult training and literacy, wellness and health, to cultural and informal adult learning, and even travel and tourism education. Colleges of education must strategically and systematically capture regional, national, and international demographic data to inform an intentional reflective process linked to their own identities and future orientations. This reflection will of necessity implicate hiring practices, tenure decisions, department structures, and even curricular choices.

Budget Pressure

The history, unfortunately, of many colleges of education is hardwired to the MEd as a funding source to support the broader institution, with a ubiquitous graduate degree tied to K-12 negotiated pay scales. Consequently, if that external, K-12 structure shifts dramatically, as is happening frequently across the nation, we are reacting to external changes over which we have little or no control. This begs some serious questions about the status and long-term well-being of an institution, the college of education, that is highly dependent on the decision making and political environment of another institution, K-12 Schools. Are colleges of education merely reactionary and subsidiary institutions in society, or do we hold some higher purpose, some broader vision? Budget decisions frequently belie deeper and more existential issues, and this is likely among the most important.

As colleges reflect on these budget pressures, one critical area of consideration is the ratio or balance between tenured faculty lines and adjunct faculty. It is an understatement of gargantuan proportions to say that the norm in college departments is to automatically fight for replacement of tenure lines. Nevertheless, college faculty rarely engage in frank discussions of the benefit package costs to the institution for tenured faculty, nor conduct realistic discussions about the important role that quality, experienced adjunct faculty bring to an institution. In our own college, we have instituted a professional fellows program that recognizes distinguished and high performing adjunct faculty with annual awards and recognition, and seeks to include these unique individuals in planning processes in the college. We have grown to appreciate the value to our students (and our faculty) by involving deeply experienced and competent field practitioners both in our program. These colleagues frequently have more immediate or current field knowledge than the tenured faculty, and most certainly more immediate experiences with children, parents, and policy decisions in the K-12 arena than most tenured faculty. In addition, these adjunct fellows are more cost-effective from a salary and benefit perspective, thereby freeing up institutional budgets to enhance tenure-line salary and benefits.

Certainly, there are nuances and complex issues related to the tenure and well as adjunct conversation. However, it is an excellent case example where colleges of education fail to systematically reflect on critical budget issues that could yield structural solutions to budget pressures.

Technology Pressure

Reflective faculties do not adopt every next new thing in the technology pipeline. If we do this, we fail to make durable and enduring decisions that improve the curriculum over time, in favor of faddishness. Colleges of education are feeling the competitive pressure of online delivery of courses. Without asking hard questions about online courses versus face to face courses, and the benefits and challenges of each of these types of instructional methods in various contexts and with various types of students, we seem to be racing toward "online everything" because "that's what students want." When do we ask basic questions, and seek answers to these questions, concerning appropriate instructional methods tied to specific content and cognitive tasks? When do we try to match learner needs with online versus face to face realities? In short: are we reflecting on the teaching learning process in conjunction with the technology questions? Technology is a tool that should be adopted from a resolute determination of vision, mission, and objectives. Our objective is not to offer online courses. Our objective is to prepare education professionals. Sometimes the two issues go together. We should always know when this is and is not the case, however.

A systematic application of the event path for reflection to technology discussions should require the college to associate learning outcomes for coursework to instructional approaches that can be enhanced by technological resources and tools. But beyond this, and perhaps more strategically, colleges should seek information from technology-focused communities that may change the nature of, or the identification of, learning outcomes themselves. What if our learning outcomes are essentially tied to or derived from a technological world that is dated, archaic, or simply does not exist any longer? What if technology, to reverse the order of that sentence, is creating a world of practice, or culture, of social reality that is fundamentally different from the world in which we as professors think and practice? Is it possible that the curricular reality to which we are oriented is no longer the reality of the society in which we are situated? To the degree that this reality exists or is emerging, our relevance and our future is at risk.

However, and this is no small aside: what if this visionary and all-encompassing technological reality is more smoke and mirrors, is more sales pitch, and is in fact a massive distraction and misdirection? More than one modern philosopher and theorist of culture has suggested that the trappings of modernist technology have in fact subtracted something tangible and important from society. More than once have we heard the suggestion that technological complexity is stripping our humanity, and that appropriate push-backs to the technological wonderkinds and advocates is needed and necessary. The reflective college is going to seek historical, serious, and thoughtful balance in assimilating technology, to strike a mix between modernism and authenticity, between efficiency and effectiveness, and between the "bells and whistles" of technology, and the time-tested, tried-and-true effectiveness of good, solid teaching ability and content knowledge embedded in a personable, affable and winsome professor.

Globalization

The emergence of the interconnected, global world should instigate in any informed institution, a period of reflection toward finding its own place in this emerging world. In short: those essential aspects of identity that derive from place are being challenged by a world culture that is, in many ways, place-less. From recruiting international students, to sending American students abroad, from negotiating a nuanced reaction to neoliberal corporate orthodoxies and social justice positions, to providing for civic engagement and citizenship values in society: how does the college of education develop its stance as a community of stakeholders, i.e. students, faculty, adjunct faculty, administrators, and alumni alike? It is ironic that the work of iconic figure John Dewey is enjoying a resurgence of interest, particularly his constructions of national citizenship and democracy, in a world where national identity is increasingly deconstructed in favor of neoliberal corporate orthodoxies. We live in a world where national boundary lines on maps are being erased in favor of ethnic boundary lines, biological habitat lines (or migration boundaries), language boundaries, economic zones—and a host of other mapping strategies. Individual nations increasingly group themselves (the Eurozone, the Organisation for Economic Co-operation and Development, the G6, G7, G20, G0, etc.) around economic identity. In this interconnected, global world, what are the constructions of citizenship and identity which bind together students in classrooms, classrooms in schools, schools and communities, and on through the continuum of organizational complexity? These are, in an overly simplistic way of speaking, challenging times for educators.

Into this mix we throw the college of education and its faculty, specifically tasked with preparing professional educators and administrators to build community and social identity within the formal and informal curricula of schooling. At the risk of overgeneralizing: can we say that requiring students to take a course in "global studies" or a 2-week study trip to the cathedrals of Europe simply doesn't cut it. The reflective college of education will seek to determine the multiple impact and implications of the globalizing event, and deeply consider interrelationships between the foundations of education and the postnational world. How do we instill within our students a deep appreciation of global culture, heightened values for diverse perspectives, cultures, languages, and lifestyles, while simultaneously appreciating and maintaining constructive connections to and appreciation for American ideals, values, history, and place in the world? Clearly, this is not a simple task, and will require greater investment of thought and energy than a new course, a revised course, or an additional sentence added to a college mission statement.

Academy Issues

Finally, beyond the abstract questions of theory and practice in the field of education, at the end of the day a college of education is in fact a college within a broader institutional context. We hire personnel, we evaluate and provide professional development for personnel. We have assessment and curriculum control and development systems. We assess and seek accreditation for our programs. We manage our behaviors with policy and procedures (and frequently say bad things about these!) We provide support services to our students. In the day to day doing of our business, are we asking reflective questions that link individual and collective experiences with our processes to effective and efficient outcomes of these processes? Can we learn to be better in behavioral and existential terms as an administrative unit?

Further, colleges of education do not exist in a vacuum in higher education. We are not the only citizen in the higher education community. What is the relationship between our college and the other colleges on campus? Are we colleagues of and with faculty in other colleges? If so, how do work together with them? How do we demonstrate institutional "neighborliness" to paraphrase our late hero, Fred Rogers. Too frequently, colleges of education (and we are certainly not alone here) develop self-centric views of the higher education universe. We grow to view our own mission (we are about saving the world, right?) as somehow superior to the concerns of our sister colleges. And while this is explicable from human nature, it does not lend itself nor support the kind of intercollegial atmosphere that we need in a period where everyone and every part of the higher education enterprise seems under sustained attack.

The reflective college of education is going to intentionally connect with and to its sister colleges, being aware of the efforts of colleagues across campus, recognizing accomplishments, assisting where and when we can. We were privileged, at our institution, this past year to see our ladies basketball team make it all the way to the final two game, playing for the national championship. Although we did not win that game, it was a magnificent "win" for our university community—faculty, staff and students. At the April meeting of our college of education, in response to a faculty suggestion, our dean invited the women's basketball team and coach to our college meeting. The college presented vases of flowers (in purple and gold!) to every young woman on the team, and to the coach. We took a full hour to let every student athlete on that team introduce herself, share about her major, and share what it was like to play for the national championship. We applauded the accomplishments of our athletic department, our athletes, and our students. It was a "first" in the life of our institution: an academic college recognizing a sports team in this expanded way. This was a small thing, and yet the positive repercussions across campus continue many months later. The reflective college is going to seek these opportunities to build intercollegiate relationships, and to seek cross-campus bridge building.

PART 2: MICROLEVEL

Moving from the social or community level, where the university and college intersect with broader societal pressures, we now focus within the college of education: What does it look like when a reflective faculty as a group or a reflective college implements its key functions following and using the reflective path that we have outlined across this text? As we considered this question, we perceived five areas which constitute an encompassing subset of much of our colleges' faculty activity or college-level business and which could be greatly facilitated by reflective processes. We discuss these below.

Curriculum Development and Management

If we are a reflective college, what does the processes of curriculum development and management look like? Following the pathway outlined in this text: our first step is identifying the current curriculum, being familiar with the curricular offerings and the rationale for these offerings. Next, we should be regularly documenting the lived experience of our curriculum: what are we doing, what is happening in classrooms with students? What evidences are we collecting that visualize the "event" of the formal and informal curriculum of the college of education? Are we using these evidences to analyze and make decisions about the effectiveness and efficiency of our curriculum so as to be prepared to make changes to that curriculum in a thoughtful, evidence-driven way?

In our state (Ohio) we are in the throes of a substantive restructuring of the college of education curriculum for advanced (graduate) programs. The state board of education has adopted a licensure structure that has substantially decreased the demand for MEd degrees, long the bread and butter of colleges of education in the state, and consequently of their universities. This has resulted in some cases in dramatic downturns in enrollment and revenue, creating in some institutions budgetary crises.

In this environment, the pressure to innovate in curriculum has many colleges looking well beyond the traditional borders of K-12 licensure to identify new markets for its tenured knowledge base and skill set. Some of these efforts will prove futile, but some are likely to be truly innovative and will help reimagine the colleges of education as academic entities within their universities, and potentially within society. Reflection seems to be a tool to best connect the history (the event) with the future (the changed or new event) in an informed and reasoned manner.

Faculty Evaluation, Development, and Promotion and Tenure Processes

If we are a reflective college, how do we go about designing and managing a system to evaluate faculty, as well as a system to provide development opportunities individualized to faculty needs and ambitions? Further, is authentic reflection embedded in the promotion and tenure process such that faculty are capturing supporting evidence that documents formative events in their early careers adequately? Following the pathway established in this text, a reflective faculty evaluation system should seek a community consensus on what constitutes evidences, on what rubrics are applied to the evidence, and on what parts of the career require visualization through evidence. Our experience in our own, and in looking at select other institutions, is that most promotion and tenure guidelines adequately describe the boundary categories (teaching, research, service) from which accomplishments should be document. It seems, however, that as one drills down into the systems, they become less precise in explaining what constitutes robust evidence, and the systems become less cohesive and clear in rubrics which assess this evidence.

We believe that embedding reflective processes into these systems can help with clarity, and can enhance the developmental nature of these systems (and we make an assumption here that the best promotion and tenure systems should indeed be truly developmental. Our own college system does "require" reflection in the portfolios, but in our own experiences, and in reviewing select examples provided us by colleagues, these "reflections" are generally detailed summaries, and frequently fail to synthesis and describe individual learning, the cognition stages of reflection we discussed in the book, and detailed descriptions of the events themselves that create the data analyzed in these portfolios. In short, reflection might shift the process from one that is more reactive, to external appearances and requirements, to one that is proactive, and representative of authentic adult learning and development.

Assessment Systems

For most colleges of education, compliance with National Council for Accreditation of Teacher Education and regional accrediting agencies has created highly complex assessment systems. These systems at the very least force the expenditure of substantive energy and budget resources. Leaving aside the questions of quality and utilization of the outcomes of these assessment systems, the inputs alone should drive a commitment to high quality and maximum use of the results of the unit level and program level assessments in the college of education. Yet, our observations, both in our own college and in others, is that there remains space for improving our use of assessment systems, and for enhancing faculty and administration commitment to use of the results of these systems to improve the learning experiences for students and the attainment of learning outcomes by students.

Reflection is, as we have written previously, fundamentally an assessment system. It attempts to create within the individual or the college learning from experience, linked to belief, and actualized in future planning and effort to improve performance. Reflection acknowledges that charts of data, numerous though they be, must describe authentic events authentically. These data must evidently describe to faculty in the college the realities of day to day accomplishments, and must be viewed as important. Critically, assessment data must be intellectually challenged, critiqued, debated, and discussed by individuals who were existentially tied to the events the data describe. The outcome of this intellectual effort must be tied sequentially to individual commitments to future effort. Short of this, assessment is falling short of its worthy promise for systems improvement in a fundamentally progressive field.

Management and Administrative Systems

All too often, the business of college administration sacrifices principle to pragmatism. Given the work load of college administration, few go into this field without a deep commitment to the institution and a calling to "do their part" as a service commitment. The financial rewards, frankly, are insufficiently motivating or rewarding to offset the grinding pace of meetings and reports. One of us (Walters) spent a year as a department chair. All of the endowment support in the world could not convince him to do that again. In theoretical terms, the extrinsic rewards are not substantial enough to offset the intrinsic costs.

We believe that reflection offers a path to analyze and reconceptualize college administration. To move from *is it working*, to *is this the best or most efficient way to make it work?* If we were to treat the entire structure of college administration as an event, an historical occurrence, and describe it in authentic terms, using a full portfolio of reflective tools to capture data to use in this description. We wonder if we could arrive at a different type of reward systems or structure, one based, for example on service or flex time or shared administrative positions? Perhaps administrative postings could become task-based contracts instead of position-linked job descriptions: treated more like consulting assignments for faculty and less like artificial hierarchies or bureaucracies. It may be that a serious attempt to reflect on the current administrative designs may reveal new possibilities for constructing management systems more rewarding to the individuals who perform the work, and consequently more effective for the various stakeholders in the college community.

Student Services and Support

Finally, who are our students: Traditionally, because of the age of college students, we have avoided the metaphor of students as our "children" as in: *in loco parentis*; but are they our clients, our subjects, our customers? What is the stance, if you will, of ourselves as a college or as individual faculty members toward students in how we respond and react to their needs and requests? Are we asking students on a regular basis "who are you? what are your needs?" Is our task, fundamentally, making students happy, or is our task, fundamentally, pushing them if necessary to a higher level of capability and academic strength even if that makes them very unhappy for a time?

The reflective college faculty is going to capture evidences in multiple ways that describe and document its practices and interactions with students, individually and corporately. What does it look like, for example, to experience our registration system as a student? What is the perception of tuition levels versus costs for room and board? What is the perception of adjunct faculty held by students? Do they disaggregate adjunct and regular faculty? How do students interpret issues of academic rigor and course requirements, and balance these with complex lives, employment and economic pressures? These and other questions in this context get at the core of how we are serving students well within the vision of our college.

Some, perhaps most, college faculty resist the merchandising and sales language of customer and product/student and course. Yet, social pressures on the institution and on families are increasingly reducing the discourses of higher education to nothing more than those cold, hard terms. We are selling access to a licensed profession to young people who are obtaining mortgages to pay for these degrees and licenses. There are macroeconomic realities to the flow of the workforce in education professions, and more than one state and college has found itself with surpluses of prepared teachers versus the jobs available. How do students perceive the fairness of this reality? What do colleges do to advise students about these issues early in their academic careers? Are we comfortable with degrees of macroeconomic planning in our institutions that may suggest that fewer students may hurt the bottom line, but may be the ethical choice given the students' debt loads and potential for employment?

The reflective institution is going to identify appropriate data to describe the experiences of students associated with the institution, and use this information to build well-rounded systems to sustain and support the students from admission through graduation and employment. Clearly, current trends in national higher education policy are very much pressing in this direction. Graduation rates, market needs for specific degrees, success rates of graduates: all of these are becoming pertinent to faculty decision making in ways that impact faculty space.

It seems clear, in reviewing these five college level issues (curriculum, promotion and tenure, management, assessment, and student services), that reflective processes that capture data through multiple tools, seek complex descriptions of college systems. Using these data, form and test tentative solutions to challenges while sustaining effective practices, and empower and embolden decisive breaks with past, ineffective practices, can help us to recapture a dynamism in our colleges that seems to have been lost. Nevertheless, all of this promise seems dependent on what the individual professor is able to find in his or her own self with respect to personal reflection on practice.

PART 3: PERSON LEVEL AND CONCLUSIONS

How do the particular problems experienced by individual faculty members, and selectively voiced in the opening stories to some of our chapters, resolve when immersed in a reflective environment? It does not seem necessary for us to extend this final section to great length, as we have explored most of these individual level observations across the various chapters of the book. We choose instead to take a more literary or perhaps philosophical level in our final comments and conclusion.

The novelist E.M. Forster, writing in the years overlapping with the Great Wars of Europe, World Wars I and II, developed a powerful essay entitled *Two Cheers for Democracy* (Forster, 1962) as a response to his observations of the real collapse of his world and its institutions. Coming on the heels of the three great revolutions (American, French, and Russian), and the collapse of the European monarchy into the modern nation-state system, realized through the near complete destruction by bombing by the nations and empires of the Allies and Axis parties, Forster had little cause for optimism. Nevertheless, he found the ideas and the voice to enunciate his own vision for building a better world. It would not be one of believe, except in the belief of the power of the individual to seek excellence. In a passage in this essay subtitled *What I Believe*, he writes:

> I believe in an aristocracy ... not an aristocracy of power, based upon rank and influence, but an aristocracy of the sensitive, the considerate and the plucky. Its members are to be found in all nations and classes, and all through the ages, and there is a secret understanding between them when they meet. They represent the true human tradition, the one permanent victory of our queer race over cruelty and chaos. (para. 13)

For Forster, these aristocrats were just individual men and women, not monarchs. Not governors. Not wealthy. Not even brilliant. But they were men and women who shared a commitment to authenticity, to exceptional conduct and performance across all manner of human effort. They were men and women committed to live beyond the unquestioned, unreflective, unexamined life of the mediocre masses with whom they rubbed shoulders.

To contextualize this to our current discussion, these were professors who would not be satisfied with meeting the minimums, with obtaining average success rates, with teaching to anyone's curve. These would be professors who would seek always to learn from personal experiences—with a deep commitment to avoid the mistakes of the past while striving for new successes, new vistas from which to view the world of practice.

This is the promise of reflective practice to the individual professor. And as individual professors engage, the concentric circles of influence engendered by these individual men and women will converge to empower the college collectively to press back against the forces in society that would undo or confound its efforts. This is the promise of reflection.

REFERENCES

Allard, C., Goldblatt, P., Kemball, J., Kendrick, S., Millen, K. J., & Smith, D. (2007). Becoming a reflective community of practice. *Reflective Practice, 8*(3), 299-314.

Amobi, F. A. (2003). Finding and speaking their own voices: Using an online survey to elicit pre-service teachers' reflectivity about educational beliefs. *Reflective Practice, 4*(3), 345-360.

Anderson, T., & McGreal, R. (2012). Disruptive pedagogies and technologies in universities. *Journal of Educational Technology and Society, 15*(4), 380-389.

Annetts, S., & Kell, C. (2009). Peer review of teaching embedded practice or policy-holding complacency? *Innovations in Education and Teaching International, 46*(1), 61-70.

Andreu, R., Canos, L., de Juana, S., Manresa, E., Rienda, L., & Tari, J. (2003). Critical friends: A tool for quality improvement in universities. *Quality Assurance in Education, 11*(1), 31-36.

Apple, M., Kenway, J., & Singh, M. (2005). *Globalizing education: Policies, pedagogies, and politics.* New York, NY: Peter Lang.

Arner, D. (1972). *Perception, reason, and knowledge: An introduction to epistemology.* Glenview, IL: Scott Foresman.

Atkins, S., & Murphy, K. (1995). Reflective practice. *Nursing Standard, 9*(45), 31-37.

Atkinson, R. C., & Shiffrin, R. M. (1968). Human memory: A proposed system and its component processes. In K. Spence & J. Spence (Eds.), *The psychology of learning and motivation.* Oxford, England: Academic Press.

Bagnall, R. G. (2006). Lifelong learning and the limits of tolerance. *International Journal of Lifelong Education, 25*(3), 257-270.

Baudrillard, J. (1994). *Simulation and simulacra* (S. Faria Slaser, Trans). Ann Arbor, MI: University of Michigan Press. (Original work published 1981)

Bell, M. (2001). Supported reflective practice: A programme of peer observation and feedback for academic teaching development. *The International Journal for Academic Development, 6*(1), 29-39.

Benjamin, W. (1934). *Art in an age of mechanical reproduction.* Retrieved from www.marxists.org/references

Bernacchio, C., Ross, F., Washburn, K., Whitney, J., & Wood, D. (2007). Faculty collaboration to improve equity, access, and inclusion in higher education. *Equity and Excellence in Education, 40*, 56-66.

Birmingham, C. (2003). Practicing the virtue of reflection in an unfamiliar context. *Theory into Practice, 42*(3), 188-194.

Boud, D., Keogh, R., & Walker, D. (Eds.). (1985). *Reflection: Turning experience into learning.* London, England: Kogan Page.

Boyd, E., & Fales, A. (1983). Reflective learning: Key to learning from experience. *Journal of Humanistic Psychology, 23*(2), 99-117.

Boyer, E. (1990). *Scholarship reconsidered: Priorities of the professoriate.* Princeton, NJ: The Carnegie Foundation for the Advancement of Teaching.

Bransford, J. D., Brown, A. L., & Cocking, R. R. (Eds.). (1999). *How people learn: Brain, mind, experience, and school.* Washington DC: National Academy Press.

Brookfield, S. (1987). *Developing critical thinkers: Challenging adults to explore alternative ways of thinking and acting.* San Francisco, CA: Jossey-Bass.

Brookfield, S. (2000). Transformative learning as ideology critique. In J. Mezirow and Associates (Eds.), *Learning as transformation* (pp. 125-150). San Francisco, CA: Jossey-Bass.

Burbank, M. D., & Kauchak, D. (2003). An alternative model to professional development: Investigations into effective collaboration. *Teaching and Teacher Education, 19*, 499-514.

Busher, H., & Saran, R. (Eds.). (1995). *Managing teachers as professionals in schools.* London, England: Kogan Page.

Butler, D. (2004). Collaboration and self-regulation in teachers' professional development. *Teaching and Teacher Education, 20*(5), 435-455.

Calderhead, J. (1992). The role of reflection in learning to teach. In L. Valli (Ed.), *Reflective teacher education: Cases and critiques* (pp. 139-146). Albany, NY: State University of New York.

Campoy, R. (2000). Teacher development: Fostering reflection in a post structural era. *Contemporary Education, 71*(2), 34-35.

Choulier, D., Picard, F., & Weite, P. A. (2007). Reflective practice in a pluridisciplinary innovative design course. *European Journal of Engineering Education, 32*(2), 115-124.

Ciprut, J. V. (2008). *The future of citizenship.* Cambridge, MA: MIT Press.

Clegg, S., Tan, J., & Saeidi, S. (2002). Reflecting or acting? Reflective practice and continuing professional development programmes in higher education. *Reflective Practice, 3*, 131-146.

Cochran-Smith, M. (2003). Inquiry and outcomes: Learning to teach in the age of accountability. *Teacher Education Practice, 15*(4), 12-34.

Cochran-Smith, M., & Lytle, S. (1992). Communities for teacher research: Fringe or forefront. *American Journal of Education, 100*, 298-324.

Corcoran, C. A., & Leahy, R. (2003). Growing professionally through reflective practice. *Kappa Delta Pi, 40*(1), 30-33.

Corcoran, T. B. (1995). *Transforming professional development for teachers: A guide for state policymakers.* Washington DC: National Governors' Association.

Cross, K. P. (1981). *Adults as learners: Increasing participation and facilitating learning.* San Francisco, CA: Jossey-Bass.

Dale, J. L. (2005). Reflective judgment: Seminarians' epistemology in a world of relativism. *Journal of Psychology and Theology, 33*(1), 56-64.

Danielson, L. (2008). Making reflective practice more concrete through reflective decision making. *The Educational Forum, 72*, 129-137.

Darling-Hammond, L., & Sykes, G. (1999). *Teaching as the learning profession: Handbook of policy and practice*. San Francisco, CA: Jossey-Bass.

Day, C. (1993). Reflection: A necessary but not sufficient condition for professional development. *British Educational Research Journal, 12*(1), 83-93.

DeBruin-Parecki, A., & Henning, J. E. (2002). Using reflective conversations as a tool for constructing meaningful knowledge about classroom practice. *Catalyst for Change, 31*(3), 16-20.

DeWaters, J. N., & Baiocco, S. A. (1998). *Successful college teaching: Problem-solving strategies for distinguished professors*. Boston, MA: Allyn & Bacon.

Dewey, J. (1933). *How we think: A restatement of the relation of reflective thinking to the education process*. Boston, MA: D. C. Heath and Company.

Ebert, E. K., & Crippen, K. J. (2010). Applying a cognitive-affective model of conceptual change to professional development. *Journal of Science Teacher Education, 21*, 371-388.

Eigenberger, M., Critchley, C., & Sealander, K. (2007). Individual differences in epistemic style: A dual-process perspective. *Journal of Research in Personality, 41*(1), 3-24.

Ellsworth, J. Z. (2002). Using student portfolios to increase reflective practice among elementary teachers. *Journal of Teacher Education, 53*(4), 342-355.

Evans, N. (1985). *Post educational society: Recognizing adults as learners*. London, England: Croom Helm.

Fedler, R., & Silverman, L. (1988). Learning and teaching styles in engineering education. *Engineering Education, 78*(7), 674-681.

Feiman-Nemser, S., & Parker, M. B. (1992). *Mentoring in context: A comparison of two U. S. programs for beginning teachers*. East Lansing, MI: National Center for Research in Teacher Learning.

Feinstein, B. C. (2004). Learning and transformation in the context of Hawaiian traditional ecological knowledge. *Adult Education Quarterly, 54*(2), 105-120.

Felder, L. (2003). Teacher reflection in the hall of mirrors: Historical influences and political reverberations. *Educational Researcher, 32*(3), 16-25.

Fenwick, T. (2001). Inside out of experiential learning: Fluid bodies, co-emergent minds. In R. Edwards, J. Gallacher, & S. Whittaker (Eds.), *Learning outside the academy: International research perspectives on lifelong learning* (pp. 42-55). New York, NY: Routledge.

Ferry, N., & Ross-Gordon, J. (1998). An inquiry into Schon's epistemology of practice: Exploring links between experience and reflective practice. *Adult Education Quarterly, 48*(2), 98-112.

Forster, E. M. (1962). *Two cheers for democracy*. New York, NY: Harcourt, Brace and World.

Foster, W. (1986). *Paradigms and promise: New approaches to educational administration*. Amherst, NY: Prometheus Books.

Freire, P. (1973). *Education for critical consciousness*. New York, NY: Seabury Press.

Freire, P. (1993). *Pedagogy of the oppressed*. New York, NY: Continuum.

Friedman, A. A. (2004). The relationship between personality traits and reflective judgment among female students. *Journal of Adult Development, 11*(4), 297-304.

Friedman, T. L. (2005). *The world is flat: A brief history of the twenty-first century.* New York, NY: Farrar, Straus, & Giroux.

Gelter, H. (2003). Why is reflective thinking uncommon? *Reflective Practice, 4*(3), 337-344.

Ghaye, A., & Ghaye, K. (1998). *Teaching and learning through critical reflective practice.* London, England: David Fulton.

Glenn, D. D., & Eklund, S. S. (1991, April). *The relationship of graduate education and reflective judgment in older adults.* Paper presented at the annual meeting of the American Educational Research Association, Bloomington, IN.

Gray, J. (1999). A bias towards short term thinking in threat-related negative emotional states. *Personality, Social and Psychology, 25,* 65-75.

Gregoire, M. (2003). Is it a challenge or a threat? A dual-process model of teachers' cognition and appraisal processes during conceptual change. *Educational Psychology Review, 15,* 147-179.

Grimmett, P., MacKinnon, A., Earickson, G., & Riecken, T. (1990). Reflective practice in teacher education. In R. Clift, W. Houston, & M. Pagach (Eds.), *Encouraging reflective practice in education* (pp. 239-250). New York, NY: Teachers College Press.

Guthrie, V. L., King, P. M., & Palmer, C. P. (1999). *Cognitive capabilities underlying tolerance for diversity among college students* (Unpublished manuscript).

Hammersley-Fletcher, L., & Orsmond, P. (2005). Reflection on reflective practices within peer observation. *Studies in Higher Education, 30,* 213-224.

Hardy, T. (1970). *Jude the obscure.* London, England: Heron Books.

Hatala, [Wlodarsky] R. L. (2002). *Understanding the relationship between undergraduate college of education professors' beliefs about student learning and teaching in their classroom practices* (Unpublished doctoral dissertation). Cleveland State University, Cleveland, OH.

Hatton, N., & Smith, D. (1995). *Reflection in teacher education: Towards definition and implementation.* Retrieved from http://www2.edfac.usyd.edu.au/LocalResource/Study1/hattonart.html

Hoban, G. (2000). Making practice problematic: Listening to student interviews as a catalyst for teacher reflection. *Asia-Pacific Journal of Teacher Education, 28*(2), 133-147.

Hobbs, V. (2007). Faking it or hating it: Can reflective practice be forced? *Reflective Practice, 8*(3), 405-417.

Hofer, B. K. (2001). Personal epistemology research: Implications for learning and teaching. *Journal of Educational Psychology Review, 13*(4), 353-383.

Hoffman-Kipp, P., Artiles, A., & Lopez-Torres, L. (2003). Beyond reflection: Teacher learning as praxis. *Theory into Practice, 42*(3), 248-254.

Honderich, T. (Ed.). (1995). *The oxford companion to philosophy.* New York, NY: Oxford University Press.

Hubball, H., Collins, J., & Pratt, D. (2005). Enhancing reflective teaching practices: Implications for faculty development programs. *The Canadian Journal of Higher Education, 35*(3), 57-81.

Ilacqua, J. A., & Prescott, M. E. (2003). Knowing economic theory: Applying the reflective judgment model in introductory economics. *Education, 124*(2), 368-376.

Illeris, K. (2007). *How we learn: Learning and non-learning in school and beyond.* London, England: Routledge.

Imel, S. (1992). *Reflective practice in adult education.* Columbus, OH: ERIC Clearinghouse on Adult, Career, and Vocational Education

Jarvis, P. (2006a). Beyond the learning society: Globalization and the moral imperative for reflective social change. *International Journal of Lifelong Education, 25*(3), 201-221.

Jarvis, P. (2006b). *Towards a comprehensive theory of human learning.* London, England: Routledge.

Jay, J. K., & Johnson, K. L. (2002). Capturing complexity: A typology of reflective practice for teacher education. *Teaching and Teacher Education, 18*, 73-85.

Kahn, P., Young, R., Grace, S., Pilkington, R., Rush, L., Tomkinson, B., & Willis, I. (2008). Theory and legitimacy in professional education: A practitioner review of reflective processes within programmes for new academic staff. *International Journal for Academic Development, 13*(3), 161-173.

Kajanne, A. (2003). Structure and content: The relationship between reflective judgment and laypeople's viewpoints. *Journal of Adult Development, 10*(3), 173-188.

King, P. M. (1992). How do we know? Why do we believe? *Liberal Education, 78*(1), 2-9.

King, P. M. (2000). Learning to make reflective judgments. *New Directions for Teaching and Learning, 82,* 15-26.

King, T. (2002). *Development of student skills in reflective writing.* Retrieved from http://www.osds.uwa.edu.au/_data/page/37666/Terry_King.pdf

King, P. M., & Kitchener, K. S. (1994). *Developing reflective judgment: Understanding and promoting intellectual growth and critical thinking in adolescents and adults.* San Francisco, CA: Jossey-Bass.

King, P. M., & Kitchener, K. S. (2004). Reflective judgment: Theory and research on the development of epistemic assumptions through adulthood. *Education Psychologist, 39*(1), 5-18.

King, P. M., & Shuford, B. C. (1996). A multicultural view is a more cognitively complex view. *American Behavioral Scientist, 40*(2), 153-165.

Kolb, D. (1984). *Experiential learning: Experience as the source of learning and development.* Englewood Cliff, NJ: Prentice Hall.

Korthagen, F., & Vasalos, A. (2005). Levels of reflection: Core reflection as a means to enhance professional growth. *Teachers and Teaching: Theory and Practice, 11*(1), 47-71.

Kouzes, J. M., & Posner, B. Z. (2007). *The leadership challenge.* San Francisco, CA: John Wiley and Sons.

Kouzes, J. M., & Posner, B. Z. (2010). *The truth about leadership: The no-fads, heart-of-the-matter, facts you need to know.* San Francisco, CA: Jossey-Bass.

Kuit, J., Reay, G., & Freeman, R. (2001). Experiences of reflective teaching. *Active Learning in Higher Education, 2,* 128-142.

Labaree, D. F. (2004). *The trouble with ed schools.* New Haven, CT: Yale University Press.

Leahy, R., & Corcoran, C. A. (1996). Encouraging reflective practitioners: Connecting classroom to fieldwork. *Journal of Research and Development in Education, 29*(2), 104-114.

Le Cornu, A. (2009). Meaning, internalization, and externalization: Toward a fuller understanding of the process of reflection and its role in the construction of self. *Adult Education Quarterly, 59*(4), 279-297.

Levine, A. (2005). *Educating school leaders.* New York, NY: Columbia University.

Levine, A. (2010). Teacher education must respond to changes in America. *Phi Delta Kappan, 96*(6), 19-24.

Livneh, C., & Livneh, H. (1999). Continuing professional education among educators: Predictors of participation in learning activities. *Adult Education Quarterly, 49*(2), 91-106.

Lloyd, C. (2002). Developing and changing practice in special educational needs through critically reflective action research: A case study. *European Journal of Special Needs Education, 17*(2), 109-127.

Lord, G., & Lomicka, L. (2007). Foreign language teacher preparation and asynchronous CMS: Promoting reflective teaching. *Journal of Technology and Teacher Education, 15*(40), 513-532.

Loughran, J. (1996). *Developing reflective practice: Learning about teaching and learning through modeling.* London, England: Falmer Press.

Loughran, J. (1999). *Researching teaching: Methodologies and practices for understanding pedagogy.* London, England: The Falmer Press.

Lyons, N. (2006). Reflective engagement as professional development in the lives of university teachers. *Teachers and Teaching: Theory and Practice, 12*(2), 151-168.

Macfarlane, B., & Ottewill, R. (2004). Business ethics in the curriculum: Assessment evidence from U.K. subject review. *Journal of Business Ethics, 54*(4), 339-347.

Mahnaz, M. (1997). The content and nature of reflective teaching: A case of an expert middle school science teacher. *Clearing House, 70*(3), 143-150.

Maloney, C., & Campbell-Evans, G. (2002). Using interactive journal writing as a strategy for professional growth. *Asia-Pacific Journal of Teacher Education, 30*(1), 39-50.

Marcoux, J., Brown, G., Irby, B., & Lara-Alecio, R. (2003, April). *A case study on the use of portfolios in principal evaluation.* Paper presented at the annual meeting of the American Educational Research Association, Chicago, IL.

Martinez, M. (1998). What is problem solving? *Phi Delta Kappan, 79,* 605-609.

Martinez, M. (2010). *Learning and cognition: The design of the mind.* Upper Saddle River, NJ: Merrill.

Mayer, R., & Whittrock, M. (2006). Problem solving. In P. A. Alexander & P. H. Winne (Eds.), *Handbook of educational psychology* (pp. 287-303). Mahwah, NJ: Erlbaum.

McNaught, C. (2003). Innovation and change in higher education: Managing multiple polarities. *Perspectives, 7*(3), 76-82.

Merriam, S. (2004). The role of cognitive development in Mezirow's transformational learning theory. *Adult Education Quarterly, 55*(1), 60-68.

Mezirow, J. (1991). *Transformative dimensions of adult learning.* San Francisco, CA: Jossey-Bass.

Mezirow, J. (1998). On critical reflection. *Adult Education Quarterly, 48*(3), 185-198.

Mezirow, J. (2000). Learning to think like an adult: Core concepts of transformation theory. In J. Mezirow & Associates (Eds.), *Learning as transformation* (pp. 3-34). San Francisco, CA: Jossey-Bass.

Milner, R. H. (2003). Teacher reflection and race in cultural contexts: History, meanings and methods in teaching. *Theory into Practice, 42*(3), 173-180.

Moon, J. (1999). *A handbook of reflective and experiential learning: Theory and practice.* London, England: Routledge.

Moon, J. (2004). *A handbook of reflective and experiential learning.* London, England: Routledge.

National Council for Accreditation of Teacher Education. (2008). *Revised NCATE Unit Standards in effect in fall 2008.* Retrieved from http://www.ncate.org/documents/standards/UnitStandardsMay07.pdf

Novak, J. D. (1998). *Learning, creating, and using knowledge: Concept maps as facilitative tools in schools and corporations.* Mahwah, NJ: Erlbaum.

Novak, J. D., & Gowen, D. B. (1984). *Learning how to learn.* New York, NY: Cambridge University Press.

Ormrod, J. (2004). *Human learning.* Columbus, OH: Pearson.

Pascarella, E. T., & Terenzini, P. T. (2005). *How college affects students: A third decade of research.* San Francisco, CA: Jossey-Bass.

Paulsen, M. B., & Feldman, K. A. (1995). Taking teaching seriously: Meeting the challenge of instructional improvement. *ASHE-ERIC Higher Education Reports 2,* 1-164.

Piaget, J. (1954). *The construction of reality in the child.* New York, NY: Basic Books.

Pirttila-Backman, A., & Kajanne, A. (2001). The development of implicit epistemologies during early and middle adulthood. *Journal of Adult Development, 8*(2), 81-97.

Pirttila-Backman, A. M. (1993). *The social psychology of knowledge reassessed: Toward a new delineation of the field with empirical substantiation.* Helsinki, Finland: Suomalainen Tiedeakatemia.

Platzer, H., Blake, D., & Ashford, D. (2000a). An evaluation of process and outcomes from learning through reflective practice groups on a post-registration nursing course. *Journal of Advanced Nursing, 31*(3), 689-695.

Platzer, H., Blake, D., & Ashford, D. (2000b). Barriers to learning from reflection: A study of the use of group work with post-registration nurses. *Journal of Advanced Nursing, 31*(5), 1001-1008.

Pultorak, E. G. (1993). Facilitating reflective thought in novice teachers. *Journal of Teacher Education, 44*(4), 288-295.

Quinlan, K. M., & Akerlind, G. S. (2000). Factors affecting departmental peer collaboration for college teachers' development: Two cases in context. *Higher Education, 40*(1), 23-52.

Richards, J. C. (1990). Beyond training: Approaches to teacher education in language teaching. *The Language Teacher, 14*(1), 3-8.

Rogers, C. (2002). Defining reflection: Another look at John Dewey and reflective thinking. *Teachers College Record, 104*(4), 842-866.

Rogers, E. M. (2003). *Diffusion of innovations.* New York, NY: McMillan.

Rowe, A., & Mason, R. (1987). *Managing with style: A guide to understanding, assessing and improving decision making.* San Francisco, CA: Jossey-Bass.

Russo, T. C., & Ford, D. J. (2006). Teachers' reflection on reflective practice. *Journal of Cognitive Affective Learning, 2*(2), 1-12.

Sack, J. (2005). State budgets feel pressure on many fronts. *Education Week, 24*(25), 17.

Schön, D. A. (1983). *The reflective practitioner: How professionals think in action.* New York, NY: Basic Books.

Schön, D. A. (1987). *Educating the reflective practitioner: Toward a new design for teaching and learning in the professions.* San Francisco, CA: Jossey-Bass.

Schuster, J. H. (2003). The faculty makeover: What does it mean for students? *New Directions for Higher Education, 123*, 15-22.

Schutz, A. (1967). *The phenomenology of the social world.* London, England: Heinneman.

Seibert, K. W., & Daudelin, M. W. (1999). *The role of reflection in managerial learning: Theory, research and practice.* Westport, CT: Quorom Books.

Sen, B., & Ford, N. (2009). Developing reflective practice in LIS education: The SEA-change model of reflection. *Education for Information, 27*, 181-195.

Shulman, L. S. (1987). Knowledge and teaching: Foundations of the new reform. *Harvard Educational Review, 57*, 1-22.

Slavin, R. (2011). *Educational psychology: Theory and practice.* Upper Saddle River, NJ: Pearson.

Starcke, K. (2011). Does stress alter everyday moral decision-making? *Psychoneuroendocrinology, 36*(2), 210-219.

Starcke, K., Wolf, O., Markowitsch, H., & Brand, M. (2008). Anticipatory stress influences decision making under explicit risk conditions. *Behavioral Neuroscience, 122*, 1352-1360.

Stempfle, J., & Badke-Schaub, P. (2002). Thinking in design teams: An analysis of team communication. *Design Studies, 23*(5), 473-496.

Sternberg, R. (1988). Mental self-government: A theory of intellectual styles and their development. *Human Development, 31*(2), 197-224.

Sternberg, R. (1997). *Thinking styles.* New York, NY: Cambridge University Press.

Sternberg, R., & Zhang, L. (Eds.). (2001). *Perspectives on thinking, learning, and cognitive styles.* Mahwah, NJ: Erlbaum.

Strydom, J. F., Zulu, N., & Murray, L. (2004). Quality, culture, and change. *Quality in Higher Education, 10*(3), 207-217.

Stump, S., & Donnel, J. (2002). Talking about team framing: Using argumentation to analyze and support experimental learning in early design episodes. *Design Studies, 23*(1), 5-23.

Tillman, L. C. (2003). Mentoring, reflection and reciprocal journaling. *Theory into Practice, 42*(3), 226-233.

U.S. Department of Education. (2006). *A test of leadership: Charting the future of U.S. higher education,* Washington, DC: Author.

Usher, R., Bryant, I., & Johnston, R. (1997). *Adult education and the postmodern challenge: Learning beyond the limits.* London, England: Routledge.

Vallance, M. (2006). *The impact of synchronous inter-networked teacher training in ICT integration.* Ann Arbor, MI: ProQuest.

Vallance, M. (2008). Using a database application to support reflective practice. *TechTrends, 52*(6), 69-74.

Vance, C., Groves, K., Paik, Y., & Kindler, H. (2011). *Measuring and building linear/ nonlinear thinking style balance for enhanced management education and professional practice.* Briarcliff Manor, NY: Academy of Management and Learning and Education.

Van Manen, M. (1977). Linking ways of knowing with ways of being practical. *Curriculum Inquiry, 6,* 205-228.

Vygotsky, L. S. (1996). *Thought and language.* Cambridge, MA: MIT Press.

Wadsworth, B. J. (2004). *Piaget's theory of cognitive and affective development.* Boston, MA: Pearson Education.

Walters, H. (2002). *The philosophical aims for the continuing professional education of teachers held by administrators, educational directors, program designers, and principal investigators funded by the National Sea Grant College Program* (Unpublished doctoral dissertation). The University of Southern Mississippi, Hattiesburg, MS.

Warhurst, R. (2008). Reflections on reflective learning in professional formation. *Studies in the Education of Adults, 40*(2), 176-191.

Weasmer, J., & Woods, A. M. (2003). Mentoring: Professional development through reflection. *The Teacher Educator, 39*(1), 64-75.

Willis, E. M. (2002). Promise and practice of professional portfolios. *Action in Teacher Education, 23*(4), 18-27.

Wink, J., & Putney, L. (2002). *A vision of Vygotsky.* Boston, MA: Allyn & Bacon.

Winch, C. (1998). *The philosophy of human learning.* London, England: Routledge.

Wilson, J. P. (2008). Reflecting-on-the-future: A chronological consideration of reflective practice. *Reflective Practice, 9*(2), 177-184.

Wise, R., & Rothman, R. (2010). The online learning imperative: A solution to three looming crises in education. *Alliance for Excellence in Education, 76*(3), 52-58.

Wlodarsky, R. (2005). The professoriate: Transforming teaching practices through critical reflection and dialogue. *Teaching and Learning: The Journal of Natural Inquiry and Reflective Practice, 19*(3), 156-172.

Wlodarsky, R. (2009). Promoting professional reflection: Tools that help education professionals facilitate the reflective process. *Teaching and Learning: The Journal of Natural Inquiry and Reflective Practice, 23*(3), 89-97.

Wlodarsky, R. (2010). Teacher reflectivity: Importance, origins, and tools to facilitate. In E. Pultorak (Ed.), *The purposes, practices and professionalism of teacher reflectivity: Insights for 21st century teachers and students* (pp. 211-230). Lanham, MD: Rowman & Littlefield.

Wlodarsky, R., & Walters, H. (2006). Reflective practitioners in higher education: The nature and characteristics of reflective practice among teacher education faculty. *National Forum Journal of Teacher Education, 16*(3), 1-16.

Wlodarsky, R., & Walters, H. (2007). The event path for professional reflection: The nature and characteristics of reflective practice among teacher education faculty. *Journal of Cognitive and Affective Learning, 4*(1), 25-31.

Wlodarsky, R., & Walters, H. (2010). Use of the reflective judgment model as a reference tool for assessing the reflective capacity of teacher educators in a college setting. *I-manager's Journal of Educational Psychology, 4*(1), 13-20.

Wong, S., Yung, B., Cheng, M., Lan, K., & Hodson, D. (2006). Setting the stage for developing pre-service teachers' conceptions of good science teaching: The role of classroom videos. *International Journal of Science Education, 28*(1), 1-24.

Wright, L. L. (2009). Leadership in the swamp: Seeking the potentiality of school improvement through principal reflection. *Reflective Practice, 10*(2), 259-272.

Zeichner, K. (1994). Research on teacher thinking and different views of reflective practice in teaching and teacher education. In I. Carlgren, G. Handal, & S. Vaage (Eds.), *Teachers' minds and actions: Research on teachers' thinking and practice* (pp. 9-27). Washington, DC: The Falmer Press.

Zeichner, K. M., & Tabachnick, R. B. (Eds.). (1991). *Issues and practices in inquiry-oriented teacher education.* London, England: Falmer.

Zhang, L. (2004). Thinking styles and the Eriksonian stages. *Journal of Adult Development, 18*(1), 8-17.

Zhang, L., & Sternberg, R. (2000). Are learning approaches and thinking styles related? A study of two Chinese populations. *Journal of Psychology, 134*(5), 469-489.

Zhang, L., & Sternberg, R. (2006). *The nature of intellectual styles.* Mahwah, NJ: Erlbaum.

ABOUT THE AUTHORS

Dr. Rachel Wlodarsky is an associate professor in the College of Education at Ashland University. Her primary teaching and research interests are in educational psychology, adult education, and reflective practice, as well as in the foundations of educational thought and inquiry. She also serves as a research fellow in the Center for Educational Development and Research.

Dr. Howard Walters is a professor in the College of Education at Ashland University. His teaching and research fields include human and global cultural analysis, critical theory, statistical analysis and research theory. Walters is the author of two books, several book chapters, and more than 100 published research papers and technical reports. His research has framed policy formation for two U.S. administrations. His current research and consulting efforts include projects with the National Science Foundation, the United Nations, the International Ocean Drilling Program, and the Vatican.

CPSIA information can be obtained at www.ICGtesting.com
Printed in the USA
LVOW01s1606170814

399561LV00004B/50/P

9 781623 964696